To my mother's

When my father, a Soviet Navy test pilot crashed, my mother was 31. She never remarried. Instead, she dedicated her entire life to my sister and me. Words fail to describe her devotion to the memory of our father and her loving caring for us, children.

Realizing the Heart
of
Success

Yuri Spilny

WWW.BooksToEnjoy.com

BooksToEnjoy.com
Yuri's Hill
Peppermint Meadow, HC1, Box 106
Kernville, CA 93238

Realizing the Heart of Success
(Love's Little Secret, revised)
Copyright © 2017 by Yuri Spilny

Title created by Lynn Shook
Cover designer Bernie Bernstone

For information about the book write to
gratitude@wildblue.net

Editors Jill Sloan and Katya Khellblau

ISBN-13: 978-1548559229   ISBN-10: 1548559229

Interactive Contents

Introduction	6
Talent	11
The Law of Happiness and Success	20
Realizing the Heart of Success	26
Transformation	26
True dreamers of the American dream	70
Addendum	89
Subconscious	89
Intuition	92
Spontaneous Irrevocable Decision	95
Selection	122
About the Author	135
Other books by the author	136

Ah, Love! Let's thou and I with fate conspire
To grasp this sorry scheme of things entire,
Would not we shatter it to bits – and then
Re-mould it nearer to the heart's desire!

                                      Omar Khayyam*

(*) Translation of Omar Khayyam's Rubaiyat by Edward Fitzgerald

Introduction

When the negative past that is locked in our subconscious is intentionally transformed into Love, Love with a capital 'L' takes up residence in our heart. It is in that moment lasting Happiness and true Success is realized.

Suddenly, all doors open.

I realized this truth when some time ago I came to the possession of a small fortune. At that time, I was offered to organize Russian-American Investment Symposium at Harvard University. There were eleven employees in my Moscow office, and together with the Harvard School of Government, we did several Russian-American meetings in Boston. It was a very successful venture.

Since I was the sole owner of the company, I had legal and moral right to keep the profit that over a period of five years would amount to six-seven hundred thousand dollars.

It was a quite exciting promise. Yet, there was something disturbing with the "moral" aspect of it: it did not feel exactly right. By that time, I had had almost 20 years' experience of classic meditation. Suddenly, surprising even myself, I have made the spontaneous irrevocable decision to share all the profits with my employees, which I did. Quickly I realized the joy of loving and giving is far greater than satisfaction brought by gaining and keeping.

Years later, when researching some statistics for *The Lion Moves Alone,* I came across Andrew Carnegie's dictum *He who dies rich dies disgraced.* It shocked me. Years before I had given up reading, but now I was eagerly reading Carnegie's *Autobiography* and *The Gospel of Wealth.*

In *The Gospel of Wealth,* Carnegie appeals to the rich suggesting to give all their wealth to services that would *benefit the nation and its people.* Giving away his wealth, Andrew Carnegie did not expect to get anything in return, but he was led by Love and, without asking, he was rewarded with the most precious of all life's gifts: Happiness.

In the thought that he (Ed. Andrew Carnegie) had worked for the realization of certain ideas, he discovered the secret of a serene and happy spirit, a characteristic which marked his life, especially after his retirement from business and up to the day of his death.
S.N.D. North

It is not man's greatness, as it is perceived by others that matter most to the man himself, nor his achievements. Every U. S. president is perceived as a great achiever. Henry Ford, J. P. Morgan, J. D. Rockefeller and their like are believed to be great achievers. Yet, in the absence of

Love, true Happiness eluded all these men. In the end, only true Happiness matters to a man himself and… Love.

True Happiness (Happiness with a capital 'H') is a permanent peaceful state where the mind is free from negativity and true Love (Love with a capital 'L') is the leader.

True Love is loving-kindness, compassion, understanding, and acceptance. It is our essence and is at the root of every human experience of love.

When achievement is rooted in Love, it is called true Success (Success with capital "S").

An occupation, no matter how enjoyable, will not result in Happiness; it can bring only temporary satisfaction. It is the same with your family. Only Love creates the result of Happiness that makes for the joy of an occupation, the family everlasting, and all other joys.

When Love is absent, no accomplishment regardless of its size can bring Happiness. Like sex, achievements can bring only temporary satisfaction. (True) Success is incomparably more satisfying as it is beneficial to others as well as to the creator. It is always giving, it is shared. When created without Love, success is often selfish, as only the business owners enjoy it.

Sharing of one's success brings immeasurable fulfillment.

"The more I do for others, the happier I am. The happiness and optimism I have obtained from helping others are a big part of what keeps me sane."
        Bill Ackman, The Giving People

"Living is giving. I won't deprive my family of knowing how good it feels to help those in need with some of the basics we already have…food, shelter, care and a future."
John Paul DeJoria, The Giving People

"There is nothing more satisfying and exciting than being able to positively affect people and noble causes in this world."
Dan Gilbert, The Giving People

Honoré De Balzac once said that behind every great wealth there is always a crime.

Yet, in the nineteenth century, a great phenomenon took place: Andrew Carnegie, a business tycoon who was led by Love. His unparalleled example has proved that a great wealth can be made without crime and greed behind it, and what is most important – the whole of it can be given back to people. Not only had Carnegie proved that an enormously successful business can be created with and be led by Love, he also has demonstrated that when business is led by Love, Love would bring Happiness to its owner.

When children are raised in a loving environment like Carnegie, there will be Heaven on Earth because when a child has been raised with Love there will be almost no negativity in the child's subconscious.

As a child, Stalin grew up in a poor family of the cobbler. His drunk father often beat him and his mother Keke. Josef grew to become an angry liar, a pretender and a bandit with a criminal record. Hitler was a very bright child and was popular at school but often clashed with his father over his interest in fine arts. This led to Hitler's detachment from his family and he became a reclusive, discontented, resentful child, with an unstable temperament.

When raised with Love, people will naturally embrace the idea of sharing and helping others as it is in the case of *The Giving People*. Those who were not been raised with Love as naturally reject the idea of sharing and helping others because ignorance prevails in the mind influenced by the negative subconscious past. The overwhelming majority of Americans are not raised in a loving environment. These people are not led by Love, which is the main reason for chaos in personal lives and a life of humanity.

What is the greatest title of all time? I believe it is *Gone with the Wind* because it perfectly points to the essence of the story: Great people, beautiful love… all gone with the wind of war. It also emphasizes action for the wind is forever on the move. The title also provokes some eternal questions: Why should great people die? Why should beautiful love vanish forever? With this title, there is no doubt that you are in for a breathtaking treat. I would suggest it as an example of how you may define your life's fundamental purpose: to live a beautiful life of Happiness and Success.

Exhibition of handmade art at Lake Quaroun, Egypt, 2016

Talent

In 1976, I was filming on St. Croix, Virgin Islands. On Friday evening, hungry and tired after twelve-hour shooting day, we stopped at a small cafe set on top of the cliff high above the sea. The whole structure seems to be floating as the only transparent sheets of light plastic curtains separated a cozy mahogany cafe interior from the darkening blue Caribbean leisurely reflecting crimson of the setting sun.

Suddenly, there was a sound, a song... and the feelings it evoked were incredible. I think I have never felt anything like that before... nostalgia, a little sadness with a little warmth were intertwining with love and joy, and some great unknown energy... altogether inexplicably pleasant and serene. The song was *Hotel California*. It has just begun its triumphant conquest of the world.

Recently I stumbled upon the blog and got curious with hundreds of fans arguing over the song's meaning.

Is it possible to define the meaning of the Sunset reflecting memories of the dying day in the forever rising and falling waves of the ocean?

In 2008, Don Felder described the origins of the lyrics: "Don Henley and Glenn wrote most of the words. All of us kind of drove into LA. at night. Nobody was from California, and if you drive into LA. at night... you can just see this glow on the horizon of lights, and the images that start running through your head of Hollywood and all the dreams that you have, and so it was kind of about that..."

"... kind of about that." Even a song's writer cannot define its meaning because... there is no meaning. At the same time, everyone who is listening to the song creates his or her own meaning. There are as many meanings as there are listeners, which mean... no one meaning that can be defined. Then what is there if there is no meaning? Hints, beats of memories and feelings, reflections and associations that are not clearly defined... which all together creates a very special mood, a very individual mood to each of us, corresponding with our vision and imagination....

That's *Talent*! And there are no definitions. The song is a stroke of genius. No one can describe this stroke, except... critics. A song critic is often a failed songwriter. It is the same with success coaches who are teaching success based on achievements of fortune creators. A fortune builder creates with his *Talent* a unique song called Fortune and no one can explain how he did it, even the creator himself. This is why many of *The Giving People* use words like "luck", "genes" and "being born to loving parents".

How foolish we are not to recognize what we are best fitted for and can perform, not only with ease but with pleasure, as masters of the craft. More than one able man I have known has persisted in blundering in an office when he had a great talent for the mill and has worn himself out, oppressed with cares and anxieties, his life a continual round of misery, and the result of last failure. I never regretted parting with any man so much as Mr. Kloman. His was a good heart, a great mechanical brain, and had he been left to himself I believe he would have been glad to remain with us. Offers of capital from others--offers which failed when needed--turned his head, and the great mechanic soon proved the poor man of affairs.

   Andrew Carnegie in *Autobiography*

How foolish we are not to recognize what we are best fitted for and can perform, not only with ease but with pleasure, as masters of the craft.

There are many mysteries in life that no one can solve. From life itself being a mystery to our solar system and the universe being greater mysteries... are we living in a real world or in a computer simulation? There is also something called *Talent*, which so far is an unsolved mystery that happens to be a prime reason for success in any field of life. It's important to remember that the word success (small's') identifies any success, small or large in any field when it is achieved without Love. Whereas Success (capital 'S') identifies accomplishment of any size made in any field of life when we are guided by Love.

In the chapter *True Dreamers of the American Dream: The Giving People,* you'll find some of them are using word "luck" as being one of the reasons for their success. What is luck? By some, it means being born in America, the land of opportunities; others believe luck means lucky genes or being born to loving parents... Yet, this so-called luck has nothing to do with success or Success.

In the Tao, every day something is "dropped" so it has no influence upon us... When we are in search of truth, ideally, all acquired knowledge pertinent to the human world needs to be set aside because most of it is not genuine and/or right. If your acquired knowledge would be genuine in relation to your life, you would be now led by Love and live a life of Happiness. It is impossible to evade influence of the acquired knowledge with a wishful thinking, positive thinking, and mantras or by any other means.

Mantras have no power that is often ascribed to them. The mantra was created as an aid to meditation. We may start a meditation session with a mantra in order initially to calm the mind. As mind gets calmer it is also easier to watch. Mantra cannot eliminate or neutralize any forces; it cannot break obstacles, the only awakened mind can. The mind could do this much better when it is calm and loving. In order for a mantra to become a useful aid to meditation and/or *Transformation,* it must be rooted in Love. You must believe unconditionally in the meaning you ascribe to the mantra, even as John D. Rockefeller believed in his, "I will live 100 years".

Classic meditation (see: *Classic Meditation* in *The Lion Moves Alone, with Lester's The Final Step to Freedom*) or *Transformation* will eliminate negativity as well as "disarm" an acquired knowledge that will not be erased but will lose its ability to influence. When this happens, we would be able to use any information and be not affected by it, as Love will be our only guide.

Right knowledge leads to either Classic meditation or *Transformation*. It may be a hint, teaching or a quote that will result in a sudden revelation.

Believe not because some old manuscripts are produced. Believe not because it is your national belief. Believe not because you have been made to believe from your childhood, but reason truth out, and after you have analyzed it, then if you find it will do good to one and all, believe it, live up to it and help others live up to it.

Attributed to Buddha

With *the right knowledge*, you will see things clearer. You would also perceive that in relation to success, the word luck is meaningless, as it does not define the reason behind the success; it may also be misleading implying that anyone can get lucky at creating, for example, great wealth.

People are often getting confused with definitions such as luck, success, and *Talent*. A common understanding of a big financial success, almost any success is usually attributed to luck. Yet, everyone who rose from rags to riches has created wealth because they possessed a *Talent* of creating wealth. The main reason for this confusion is *Talent's* mystery that cannot be defined.

A substance creates a major difference between definitions of luck and *Talent*. Luck has no substance. It is an empty word, which is used to compensate for a lack of knowledge of the cause. On the other hand, *Talent* has great substance behind it. Yet, the most important part of this "substance" is still a mystery, which makes *Talent* a mystery that causes people to confuse it with "luck".

Only as a distant approximation may we allude to *Talent* as being a set of special qualities, where each quality must be uniquely individual and harmonious with all other qualities in order to create a success in any field of life. The more fine-tuned and harmonious the alliance of these qualities, the greater success or Success. When most of these qualities are lacking, there is no *Talent* and there can be no success made in that field. Yet, anyone can discover his/her *Talent* and succeed in a field that is harmonious with that *Talent*.

Every *Talent* is purely individual. Every original (as opposed to inherited) great wealth has been created with a unique individual *Talent*, even like song *Hotel California* was created with a unique *Talent* or *Gone with the Wind* and *The Razor's Edge* was written by the people of great *Talent*. *Talent* cannot be acquired like skill, for *Talent* is inborn and indefinable. Yet, with Love, anyone can discover his or her *Talent*.

Andrew Carnegie, John D. Rockefeller, Henry Ford, J. P. Morgan and every other people who rose from rags to riches were born with a *Talent*. There is a degree of *Talent* as well as a quality to *Talent*. A degree of the *Talent* characterizes the size of a corresponding success, whereas quality in the *Talent* means presence or absence of Love.

Do you know of any popular song that is about violence, murder or pornography? With only a few exceptions, the songs are all about love and relationship between a man and a woman.

Why then there are so many pictures feature violence? When a song is created and it becomes popular this creation is rooted in Love; there also must be the *Talent*. People love and enjoy songs about love, they love and enjoy the subject of love more than any other subject... then why not to make movies featuring beautiful love stories that demonstrate the power of Love?

There are several reasons why despite people's loving the subject of love more than they love any other subject, the majority of films are featuring violence. The main reason, however, is the demand: the low awareness of the masses wants to get excited with violence. It will certainly change with time, with a higher level of awareness. Another reason is that some filmmakers either have no *Talent* or there is a *Talent* but it is lacking the quality of Love thus turning a filmmaker into a robot driven by the subconscious negativity.

In the absence of Love, the mind endowed with a *Talent* can become a very tricky mind. It may convince itself it can get away with murder... and it does, for we become what we believe. Yet, if a person is still sane, it will not commit the actual murder. Instead, they will express their conviction in writing a violent novel (The Godfather by Mario Puzo) or creating a violent motion picture (Chain Saw Massacre), etc. If a talented mind lost sanity, it may create a murderous philosophy, like Hitler's and Stalin's.

When a *Talent* is lacking the quality of Love, it cannot create a gifted love story. Instead, it would travel an easy way of least resistance and capitalize on people's lower nature using violence for bait. However, like any other human being, a talented filmmaker may sometimes have a glimpse of Love. When this spark of Love happens, even when Love is not yet realized, *ET* is made or a striking love story is created.

The society would praise with the same enthusiasm *ET* and *The Godfather,* and spread violence in the world.

A similar situation takes place in human life, as every human either has or lacks the quality of Love.

Nevertheless, we all possess the *Talent* to realize Love. It is usually hidden under a pile of rubble and needs to be re-discovered. Suffering, problems, disappointments, and glimpses of satisfaction will forever keep turning one after the other until the realization of Love will destroy this roller coaster.

Mozart was writing symphonies since he was five years old, which makes it obvious that *Talent* cannot be learned, thus, it cannot be emulated. No matter how hard one would try, without having the same *Talent* he will not be able to reach the supremacy of Mozart. Is it ever possible to have the same as someone else's *Talent*?

When I came to Los Angeles, my agent convinced me to audition for a part in an independent movie. I did OK, but far from being great. Then the producer invited me to his office and asked if I really want to act. I pulled myself together and said I wanted to try, but now I see I have no talent. Why, he said, you did quite well? I had to explain that I felt miserable and ashamed because I saw that I was not good enough, that acting should be a joyful performance with little or no effort, that I don't want to be just another mediocrity. He laughed, and we had a chat about the Red Empire.

eBay Chairman Pierre Omidyar launched *First Look Media* in late 2013 with the aim of presenting new forms of independent journalism. Would Pierre be able to create a great wealth of over $7 billion without having a *Talent*? What made Pierre pledge a major share of his assets to charitable causes if not Love?

What can be done when because of some unfortunate circumstances we are not able to utilize our *Talent*? When Love is realized, even if we cannot employ our *Talent*, Love will guide us to the most beneficial scenario, whether it is schooling, employment or a partnership, and enable us to create a life of Happiness.

Blood of the Lion, an ancient city lost in the Sahara Desert, Egypt

The Law of Happiness and Success

According to the records, founded almost 3000 years ago, a city called *Blood of the Lion* prospered for almost thousand years. It was built by the sea and became a well-known international seaport. Then, the sea moved away. A fleeting time of prosperity ended..., the *Blood of the Lion* was abandoned and disappeared, swallowed by the sands of the Sahara Desert. It was rediscovered only in the end of the last century.

There were many prosperous cities in ancient time. However, there is no record of people living in these cities a life of Happiness. There was never a crowd that lived a life of Happiness. Like Love, Happiness was experienced only by a handful of individuals.

Today we have information available on any aspect of life, Love, and Happiness; we also have excellent communication tools. Still, there is no Love and Happiness in the human world. Because today we have no time, we are afraid to lose, to be left behind, to be unsuccessful, etc... We live longer lives but waste them in spinning wheels and chasing shadows.

The Law of Happiness and Success is pertinent to every field of life, every vocation when our endeavors are rooted in Love.

When several decades ago I experienced an out-of-body projection, it set me on the spiritual path of meditation, yoga, and study of religions. I clearly defined my fundamental purpose: Freedom.

However, I was also making a living and had material goals to attain. This combination of the material path and spiritual often made me contemplate material success, causing an inquiry to subtly reside in the back of my mind: is there a rule that can be learned and applied, that will allow harnessing material success without losing spiritual goal of Freedom? Like most people, I believed material success is measured with money and desire for money thwarts inner growth. Yet, in my heart, I was convinced that there must be something like a formula of (true) Success and kept searching for it. When I "discovered" Andrew Carnegie, I knew I found it.

Andrew Carnegie demonstrated that when Success is created to benefit people, the creator will thrive as well as be gifted with Happiness. If Lester Levenson is a perfect example of how one finds Happiness with Love, Andrew Carnegie is an enlightening example of how Love can harmonize Happiness and wealth. When you transform your negative subconscious past into Love, you will become another great example of the one who caught two birds: Happiness and Success.

When there is no Love, there is no law of success; neither are there rules that help to create success. If there were rules, anyone would be able to learn how to create wealth. The Law of Success, which is taught to eager crowds, is a trick created in a dreamland unaware (unintentionally). It is a dead-end road because it considers neither Love nor *Talent*. Blinded by desire people believe that studying and closely following those who have risen from rags to riches, they would become as successful… and fail.

Those who have risen from rags to riches themselves were never able to explain how they did it. Volumes have been written about how to become rich. However, there is no explanation of the mechanics of the process and no method. There are only hints, some common qualities of the character, etc., which means nothing because one unique thought makes a great deal of difference.

An unknown secret lies in uniqueness of an individual emotional-thinking process, in the intensity of thoughts, in a matchless thought pattern, as it is applied to a particular business, in the ability to influence and organize cooperation of the participants, in timing and circumstances of that time, in the ability to sense a right opportunity, as well as in many other unknowns, which altogether define *Talent* that is impossible to describe, never mind – recreate. The world is changing every instance and there can be no two sets of the same circumstances or persons separated in time, except for the illusion of similarity created by the mind.

Love makes all the difference as it transforms a mythical law of success into powerful *The Law of Happiness and Success,* which is the law of Love. This law is true and it can be learned and implemented.

"Nearly twenty years ago," writes Napoleon Hill in his *Law of Success,* "I interviewed Mr. Carnegie for the purpose of writing a story about him. During the interview, I asked him to what he attributed his success. With a merry little twinkle in his eyes, he said: "Young man before I answer your question will you please define your term 'success'?"

"After waiting until he saw that I was somewhat embarrassed by his request he continued: "By success, you have reference to my money, have you not?" I assured him that money was the term by which most people measured success, and he then said: "Oh, well if you wish to know how I got my money - if that is what you call success - I will answer your question by saying that we have a mastermind here in our business, and that mind is made up of more than a score of men who constitute my personal staff of superintendents and managers and accountants and chemists and other necessary types."

If you paid attention to the above, you would surely notice Carnegie's question "By success you have reference to my money, have you not?" This question should have led Hill to ask Carnegie what he, Carnegie, meant by success, but Hill failed to ask this most important of all questions.

Today, *The Giving People* is the most powerful demonstration of the humanity's inner growth as well as

The Law of Happiness and Success. Even like Carnegie, most of *The Giving People* were brought up by caring parents, who taught them integrity and value of giving that enabled them to live in the land of reality.

Gracious nature has not been sparing with her gifts. It bestowed Love upon every human being and endowed us with the ability to resolve all things. The more loving the mind is the more appropriate are our decisions.

The Law of Happiness and Success is the law of Love. It is simple to grasp as it means to be led by Love.

> The worldly hope men put their hearts upon
> Turns ashes or it prospers and anon,
> Like snow on dusty desert's face
> Lasting a little hour or two… is gone

Relatively a few people rose from rags to riches. Not guided by Love, they experienced much suffering, many troubles, exerted great effort. They mercilessly exploited others and ended life with no Happiness. Every "captain of industry" went through this mill. This is what makes people believe that suffering is a necessary part of success. Wrong. Suffering is inevitable only in the absence of Love. Carnegie's life is the best proof of a great rise from rags to riches into an unparalleled Success that was created naturally, honestly, with no suffering. *The Giving People* are following suit.

When Love is realized, *The Law of Happiness and Success* will guarantee Happiness, regardless of the size of income, which may be not so easy for some people to grasp. Every Talent is different. When Love and Talent dictate for you to become a teacher, so be it. With Love, you will be a great teacher and will live a life of Happiness and Success. Your Success will be expressed not in millions of dollars, but in fulfillment brought by being a wonderful teacher.

I have inherited this peculiarity and have often walked from the house to the gate intending to pull a flower for my buttonhole and then left for town unable to find one I could destroy.

Sunrise at Lake Quaroun, Egypt

Realizing the Heart of Success

Transformation

Recently I asked a great number of people the same question: "What is the Heart of (true) Success?" Only two people named Love. Many thought it was hard work, others named perseverance, confidence, even connections, some believe "luck" is at the Heart of Success...

In his work, *The Republic*, the Greek philosopher Plato (c.429-347 BC) employed the allegory of a cave to describe the human condition of *resistance*. This allegory – in which humans live imprisoned in a dark cave, deep underground – is the perfect metaphor for having to live in a state of no Love.

Yet, because people are in constant change, they are capable of the most astonishing transformation. *Transformation* of one's negative past into Love is the most rewarding example of such change. Love is inexplicably a wonderful and powerful state of being. Is there any other state, anything that may be comparable to Love? Just imagine yourself all the time to experience only Love, amazing shades of Love...

When Love is absent, there is still some goodness remaining, says the Tao, humanity's well of wisdom. When goodness is gone, morality comes up. When morality is no longer present, rituals come up, which is the beginning of chaos.

Love is the radiance and the extension of Infinite Intelligence in the human world. This unusual, mysterious inexplicable state brings Happiness and transforms a human being into a Human Being.

Like water, Love is effortlessly nourishing all things. Thoughts weaken the mind, desires wither hearts... yet, when we open ourselves to Love the mind falls quiet and follows Love's lead. Open yourself to Love and trust yourself, your intuition, which is the voice of Love.

Every true saint was a loving person. Regardless of their chosen path, every one of them became free by first realizing Love. How did they do it?
Their confidence is the key.

It makes no difference what one chooses to put his confidence in. The strength of the confidence makes all the difference because the strength of the confidence enables one to transcend the ego. It may be a symbol of God, Life,

Pure mind, or Universe. Symbols do not make any difference since symbols are principles and principles are dead. A dead principle or symbol cannot help transcend egotism. A total confidence in symbol does it, confidence that is stronger and more intense than our life-long confidence in mind.

An unshakable confidence in a crocodile, a tree or your own Self will do the same job as an unshakable confidence in God or deity. Religion wants people to rely on outside means. Yet, every human imperfection is superficial and anyone may correct it himself. It is insane to transfer your innate ability to command your life to the bunch of bones or some other entity. Philippus Paracelsus, a famous Swiss alchemist, and physician, who lived in 14 century, was a great healer in his day.

He stated what an obvious scientific fact is now: "Whether the object of your faith is real or false, you will nevertheless obtain the same effects. Thus, if I believed in Saint Peter's stature as I should have believed in Saint Peter himself, I should obtain the same effects as I should have obtained from Saint Peter. That is superstition. Faith, however, produces miracles; and whether the subject of faith is true or false, it will always produce the same wonders."

He also said, "We can easily conceive the marvelous effects which confidence and imagination can produce, particularly when both qualities are reciprocated between the subjects and the person who influences them. The cures attributed to the influence of certain relics are the effects of their imagination and confidence. Quacks and philosophers know that if the bones of any skeleton were put in place of the saint's bones, the sick would none the less experience beneficial effects if they believed that they were veritable relics."

Confidence in Love is our best choice. Whether it is business or a romantic relationship, Love is the finest part of you and your best adviser.

When we transform our past into Love, negativity is gone and mind's limitations dissolve. The mind becomes obedient and Love intuitively lights our way. The limited mind will never believe it ahead of time and will build barriers of resistance in your path. Yet, as you keep transforming your past into Love, you will be more often led by Love. The more we are cleansed of negativity the sooner we fly, as we drop the heaviest load of all, the ego or mind's limitations.

You can have, be, and do whatever you will or desire, says Lester.
The only thing stopping you is the accumulation of negative thoughts and feelings, which you are subconsciously holding.
Remove these, and you remove the blocks to your accomplishing whatever you wish in life.
Remove these, and you will find love, happiness, and joy beyond your wildest dreams.
Remove these, and you are Free.

Here Lester means the *transformation* of the subconscious negativity into Love – a Supreme Releasing process. It will enable us to *have, be, and do whatever we will or desire* because it elevates us into the realm of Love and enables The Law of Happiness and Success.

There is nothing that can be done without the mind. If you wish to go beyond the limitations of your mind, you must start with making your limited mind your best friend. Lester's mind was already his best friend. However, when oblivious to his dire conditioning, Lester started his intense search, for 30 days his mind was not able to find the answers. Nevertheless, his mind brought him to a threshold, from where answers had become possible.

How did it happen?

When, at 43, Lester had a deadly heart attack, the doctor told him that he might drop dead at any time. Facing his dire condition, Lester decided either he will find the answers to *What is life? What is it all about? Is there a reason for my being here in this world, and if so, what is it?* or to take his life. He started with reading books, but within four days of his search, it hit him that if the answers could be found somewhere in an outside source, he surely would have found them long ago, since these questions had plagued him all his life. Suddenly, he saw it: the problems lie within; therefore, the answers must also be within. From that time on, his search became extremely intense.

At the end of the first month, he stumbled upon something very important, probably the most important of all questions: What is *Happiness*? Within several days of intense trial and error, Lester had his answer: *Happiness is when I love the other one, which means Happiness is a feeling within me.* If that is so, he thought, even if I cannot change my unhappy past, I could change how I *felt* about one situation or another. I could transform it into Love, which equals Happiness. That was an incredible realization! It made him feel certain he was now in the driver's seat because he could now change to Love whatever non-loving feeling he had felt in the past.

Happiness is synonymous with Love and is beyond common sense, it is beyond logic, beyond our limited mind. Yet, all of this helps us realize Love. If you read the above attentively, you would see that Lester was using logic, reason, and common sense; he was intensely using his mind. Lester's extreme intensity helped to accelerate his search. He had no distractions, he turned off his phone and TV; he was no longer concerned with his illness, even death. Such an incredibly intense search had also exhausted his emotional thinking process.

Lester started with his search for answers in the dark. He had accidentally stumbled upon the *transformation process,* which is now available to use without initial search.

When Lester's mind fell quiet, Lester was able to hear. The more extreme the intensity of the process, the sooner mind falls quiet and the higher becomes the probability of receiving an intuitive answer. Isolation creates a kind of spiritual spa because it filters out all distractions.

One who is aware makes good use of his aloneness because he intuitively knows it is a shorter path to realization of Love.

Why would people isolate themselves in deserts, in forests? They had no methods, but intuitively they knew that isolation would help them find God. Really, they were looking for a Happiness and peace, which they thought they would receive from God. Indeed, they knew the present could not be properly understood without exploring the past.

Lester was isolated for only three months from this world and people he loved and that allowed him an intense concentration. Yet, from the moment he discovered he could transform his past into Love it took Lester only one month to realize Love. Lester was searching in the dark yet we have a proven method. Depending on your determination and intensity, it may take you longer than one month to realize Love, but it will happen. It cannot be any other way.

At the same time, Lester realized that he was responsible for everything that happened to him because it all happened as result of his haphazard emotional-thinking process and subconscious negativity. All these realizations resulted from the process of logical trial and error and brought Lester to the most important step…

His entire life came up for a review as he decided to transform to Love his entire past, all past hurts, and disappointments. Today, psychologists are well aware of the tremendous influence of the subconscious past.

Lester says, *Discovering that my Happiness equated to my loving and that my thinking was the cause of things happening to me in my life gave me more and more freedom; freedom from the subconscious compulsions that I had to work, I had to make money, I had to have girlfriends. Freedom in the feeling that I was now able to determine my destiny, I was now able to control my world, lightened my internal burden so strongly that I felt there was no need for me to have to do anything. Plus, this Happiness was so great. It was a new experience for me. I was experiencing a joy that I never knew existed, never dreamed could be. So I decided, "This is so great, I'm not going to stop until I carry it all the way." I had no idea how far it could go. I had no idea how joyous a person could be. But I was determined to find out.*

In Lester's example, the uniqueness lies in his irrevocable decision, perseverance, and intensity, all of which had intensified when Lester isolated himself. All of these put Lester on the supreme path of Love.

Lester says, *"When I mixed with people, and again and again when they would do things that I didn't like and within me was a feeling of non-Love, I would immediately change that attitude to one of loving. Eventually, I got to a point where, no matter how much I was opposed, I could feel only Love."*

As Lester was transforming his past, he also shed his desires. When we reach a certain point in the process of transforming negativity to Love… when we realize that Love is real, that Love is such a beneficial and powerful force, we simply let Love shine and evaporate every bit of negativity, and every desire that is not rooted in Love.

Lester was pushed with his back against the wall. He was under the gun: he was nearly dead, but he did not try to heal his body. This is very important to understand. He made an Irrevocable Decision to find the answers. he started with healing his mind. Yet, as his mind was healed with Love, his body also healed, as if by itself.

I began to feel stronger as the weight of my pain dropped away. I was happier than I had ever been before, and I kept it going...

For Happiness, we move within. Any other goal may temporary sidetrack us by taking into an opposite direction: without. In that, we are making our choice: Happiness, and nothing else. As to your goal of Happiness and Success, it will benefit you tenfold when you will first find Happiness because Love will become your guide and you will swiftly accomplish the Success part of your goal.

There are countless triggers of irritation within and all around us and there are many hidden reasons. We may try hard to convince ourselves not to be irritable, we may use affirmations, releasing... These are helpful but temporary measures. Irritation will persist because it is nearly impossible to pinpoint its deeply buried cause(s). Only when you transform your past into Love there will be no more irritation and a trigger, any trigger will become powerless.

An affirmation can be your aid. There is a good example of affirmations used by John D. Rockefeller's "I am bound to be rich!" and "I am bound to live 100 years!" Despite ailing during the first half of his life, Rockefeller fulfilled both of his wishes. Yet, you would need Rockefeller's conviction and determination to obtain a similar effect. Yet, like it is with a *Talent*, it is impossible to measure another's determination and conviction. Your best bet would be to note the other people's examples but have your own affirmation rooted in Love. The affirmation also helps to stop mind's wondering and keep it focused on the task.

When uneducated the mind is not interested in transforming the past misfortunes into Love. It loves to talk about Love; it loves to read about Love... We may spend life collecting information about Love from scriptures, teachings, and novels. We may become an encyclopedia of Love and still not know Love. The mind will know everything about Love and will even think that it loves with true Love but something will happen, and at once, the mind will forget about Love... irritation will happen, anger will happen.

The mind loves to talk about the past; it loves to think about past success, memorable vacations, and other happy moments. Hurts and frustrations… the mind does not want to think about past sorrows, it wants to forget it, and it is successful in forgetting and entombing it deep inside. Oh no! Not again! Immediately the Resistance is on.

When transforming negativity into Love, from your earliest childhood, one by one bring to the light of the present each negative memory of distant events and perform the magic of transformations. You will soon notice how this process will begin changing your thoughts and your attitudes, your moods, your behavior. You will come to appreciate this gift and will encourage your mind to continue until the *transformation* process is completed.

You may use pictures or list of memories, events, starting from the time you remember yourself. Family albums may be used or you may simply retrospect on your past. See if you could come up with your own idea of an aid.

Use comparison. Compare, for example, negativity to a mirage in a desert. In a desert, the mirage produces an incredible display of images. If we do not recognize the mirage as an illusion, we fall under its spell, and these ever-changing ephemeral images will mislead us in our travel. However, once we see it for what it is, its influence evaporates.

It is the same with negativity and Love. When it is conditioned, not loving, the mind believes the negativity is an inseparable part of life. It is true for a dreamland but not in the world of Love. When the mind is dreaming, its conviction empowers negativity's influence, making people fall deeper under its spell. The ever-changing non-loving feelings and thoughts are forever misleading them in their journey. *Transformation* of the subconscious negativity into Love dissolves negative influence. As soon as we understand this, our vision clears and we see that in the light of Love negativity's influence evaporates like the mirage in the desert and like the mirage, it loses its power over us.

Suffering is not imagined, war and murder are real whether Love is realized or not. Yet, this negativity can exert a very powerful influence only on the minds that do not know Love. The same negativity is powerless against a mind led by Love.

There are two kinds of negativity: internal and external. With releasing, we can let go of the internal negative influence but only partially. The *transformation* will eliminate all of it and will "elevate" us into the dimension of Love. *The momentum of Love* (see below) will ensure completion of the process despite our not remembering some negative events of the past.

As to the external negativity, *transformation* renders its influence powerless because when is led by Love the mind becomes a witness. A true witness is beyond the negative influence. Indeed, it is another dimension, and when we are there, we leave this dreamland's influence behind. From there, the mind clearly sees through people and events happening in dreamland. With the realization of Love, our mind indeed becomes an impartial witness, compassionate, and understanding.

A dreamland is an individual environment created unaware, without Love. It is but a pile of concepts, ideas, thoughts, and feelings, as well as an archive containing every individual experience.

Transformation

Transformation requires the full mind's cooperation, which happens when our mind gets educated with the *right knowledge*. An educated mind's strength lies in its unwavering confidence in the unmatched benevolent power of Love. Anyone can realize Love. What we then accomplish with Love is truly wonderful, almost magical. To experience this magic we have to become loving magicians.

Indeed, some magical elements are present in the process of realization of Love. With the realization of Love, we come close to the state of Freedom, a truly magical state.

The Momentum of Love is another magic. When we are sincerely doing all we can at transforming our negative past into Love, we are literary moved to the end of the *transformation* process with the *Momentum of Love* (explained below) which finalizes it with no more effort on our part.

One of the difficulties in the process of *transformation* lies in our subconscious confusion of the true meaning of Love with a common understanding of love for example to parents, boyfriend, child, etc.

When we are about to transform into Love negative feelings for someone we do not like, immediately resistance surges and we say something like "He is a weather-beaten rat! How could I love this person!" This happens because our subconscious is constantly influencing our emotional thinking process. In this particular case, it is confusing us into using a common meaning of love instead of Love, which is compassion and understanding.

There is only one Love: a state of Love to which people attribute/create numberless shades. They are numberless because in every situation everyone's mind creates its own shade of Love congruent with qualities of the creator. As you keep transforming your past into Love these shades disappear….

There is no direct connection between the limited mind and Love. Love is beyond limited mind (beyond ignorance), it is a state of an intuitive knowing. When the mind's limitations dissolve, Love shines and there is no need for connection because our mind is now loving. Love is a changeless boundless power of the highest good. Love is an inseparable part of ourselves but the limitations of the mind have been acquired. The mind's ETP (Emotional Thinking Process) and the negative subconscious past obscure Love yet, *transformation* can be done only with the mind's cooperation. Unwavering decision to transform your entire past into Love will establish such cooperation. You may transform negativity directly into Love or you may use one of Love's attributes: acceptance, understanding, compassion, and kindness. You may also use releasing to aid *transformation* process.

Do not try to figure it out how you can love someone who "doesn't deserve" it. Throughout the *Transformation* process, keep in mind a simple thought: this *Transformation* is propelling you into a life void of negativity – into a life of Happiness and Success. Do not analyze this thought; simply keep it in the back of your mind.

It seems impossible to love someone you hate... Here is Lester's approach to Dr. Schulz: "<u>The point is not whether he deserves love. The point is can you do it? Is it possible</u>

<u>to simply change a feeling of hatred into a feeling of love – not for the benefit of the other person but for yourself?"</u> This is a good example of logic and common sense. Contemplate it as you begin your *transformation* process: there is much meaning and power in it.

Keep this approach in mind throughout the entire process: you Love not for the benefit of another person, but for your own benefit. Yet you will be able to benefit many people when you transform your past into Love.

These powerful lines will enable you instantly transform almost every negativity, past and present. When you have troubles, apply acceptance and understanding. Imagine looking into that person's eyes... If associated negative emotions come up let it go and let perfection be, knowing Love is perfection... Keep it in mind: you are doing it for your own benefit.

Lester's suggestion is powerful and direct. Always try it first. There are no two situations or people alike. Dr. Schulz's was not a negative event; it was made negative by Lester's anger, which blinded him. Another person may be a much more complicated negative situation where that person caused hundreds of thousands civilian deaths; American soldiers killed and wounded; the collapse of the US economy; endorsement of torture; and so on. This man is much harder to deal with than with Dr. Schulz.

It would be against our nature to love people like Bush, Cheney, Lenin, and Hitler and it is not necessary. Transform into Love to humanity and life every negative emotion associated with this kind of people and events. Keep in mind, indifference is a cover for a deeply hidden negative attitude. If we have negative feelings towards any person – we are not in a state of the realized Love. When

Love is realized it celebrates the death of all negativity we had within. A (true) Love is not an emotion; it is expressed through its properties of understanding, acceptance, compassion, and kindness. When it comes to deeply negative situations, do not use the word love, instead, utilize Love's properties.

When your entire past was transformed into Love, what is left? At that point, you will not be able to experience negative emotions no matter what kind of person or event you are facing, yet you will see clearly through people and events for you will be forever anchored in the state of Love.

The Momentum of Love

Obviously one cannot transform 100% of the past into Love, as we do not remember many past events. However, there is *The Momentum of Love*. Amazingly, it is getting enforced when we have earnestly transformed everything we remember. At that moment, Love overwhelms the unremembered part of the subconscious past and burns off the rest of the negativity, thus instantly making *transformation* process complete. The timing cannot be determined as it depends on individual factors.

Lester mention, when we release all we can, the rest is completed on its own. Interestingly, *The Momentum of Love* also is ruling enlightenment in meditation: after many a hundred of hours of intense meditation, suddenly, happens the Samadhi that banishes all remaining negativity together with the influence of all remaining concepts. It "lifts" one beyond the conscious and subconscious mind into an unknown, indescribable state where the magic of meditation is instantly completed. Whether it is Samadhi or *transformation*, the shock of completion is so powerful it will "keep" one immersed in the state of Love for the rest of one's life.

Transformation is a creative process. As in meditation, we must learn how to be our own masters. Nothing can help us better than persistent practice.

Fully enjoy the wonder and beauty of each instant, and the future will take care of itself. As you enjoy each present moment completely, transform into Love anything that is not that joy and you may get into the world of Love this way.

Lester's example with Dr. Schulz is encouraging.
"First," he asked himself, "was I experiencing a lack of love that day?"
"Yes," he answered aloud. "Nobody gave a damn about me, not the nurses, not the orderlies, not even Dr. Schultz. They did not care. As sick as I was, they threw me out, sent me home to die so they would not have to watch one of their failures. Well, the hell with them. They can all go to hell." He was shocked at the vehemence in his voice. His body trembled with rage and he felt weak. He really hated the doctor. He could feel it burning in his chest. "Oh, boy," he thought," this sure isn't love."

"Well, can I change it?" he asked. "Is it possible to turn it into love for the doctor?"
"Hell, no," he thought, "Why should I? What did he ever do to deserve any love?"
"That's not the point," he answered himself. "<u>The point is not whether he deserves love. The point is can you do it? Is it possible to simply change a feeling of hatred into a feeling of love – not for the benefit of the other person but for yourself?</u>"

As the thought crossed his mind, he felt something break loose in his chest. A gentle easing, a sense of dissolving, and the burning sensation was gone. He did not trust it at first. It seemed too easy, so he pictured again the scene with Dr. Schultz in the hospital. He was surprised to find that it brought only a mild feeling of resentment rather than the previous intense burning hatred. He wondered if he could do it again.

"Let's see," he thought, "what did I just do? Ah, yes. Can I change this feeling of resentment into a feeling of love?" He chuckled as <u>he felt the resentment dissolve in his chest. Then it was totally gone and he was happy.</u>
"Doctor Schultz, you son-of-a-gun," he said, grinning, "I love you.""

This is a very important point: "<u>The point is not whether he deserves love. The point is can you do it? Is it possible to simply change a feeling of hatred into a feeling of love – not for the benefit of the other person but for yourself?</u>" Lester has discovered this deeply meaningful key. Make sure you grasp this meaning, which will make your sailing to Love much smoother.

It is impossible to get down to the cause of every negative emotion because the cause may have nothing to do with a current situation. It is possible the actual cause was created when you were only three years old. Not too many people would be able to remember what happened at that age. Simply remembering does not reach most our very early experiences because we had them before we had language. A small child would have no idea of the cause of the pain, even less so it would be able to explain it. The older we become the deeper these early negative memories are buried in the subconscious.

Year after year says Dr. Jack Lee Rosenberg in his book *Body, Self, Soul and Sustaining Integration*, the sealed-off irritant blocks the free flow of energy through the body and it may restrict the free range of feelings. The more painful the initial wound the tighter is the muscular defense and the less it is accessible. Releasing cannot reach that far, but *Transformation* will. Our conscious effort of *Transformation* may not reach that deep either, yet *The Momentum of Love* will eradicate remaining negative causes.

When jealousy or anger overwhelms us, though not dealing with the cause, releasing would be most effective at this very moment of the flaming emotion. Did you ever try to release an overwhelming emotion at its peak? An impossible task. If you can do it, instantly you will be free. We always "forget" releasing when we are under influence of the powerful negative feelings. We remember about releasing later and "later" releasing becomes not nearly as effective as at the time of rage.

However, even without having a sound witnessing experience, we can literary witness a past event and deal with corresponding emotions almost at arm's length. When these "past" emotions arise, they are usually not nearly as powerful as at the time of that distant event and are nearly not as powerful as those experienced in daily life. Thus, they are much easier to release via transforming them into Love.

Believe not because some old manuscripts are produced. Believe not because it is your national belief. Believe not because you have been made to believe from your childhood, but reason truth out, and after you have analyzed it, then if you find it will do good to one and all, believe it, live up to it and help others live up to it.

In the process of *transformation* measure up negative situations against this quote to understand that unless *transformed* into Love, they will keep hampering your progress.

With *transformation* come two benefits. We permanently eliminate hidden causes of negative emotions and lose the ability to become angry, greedy, fearful, apathetic, proud, etc. It will all be gone together with irritation, annoyance and other negativity. Occasionally, we may still go off track and experience hints of some of these negative emotions. Yet, we can now instantly let them go – transform into Love and usually – at their root and before they fully manifest themselves.

When we realize Love, we are not yet free as Freedom means an unencumbered peace. However, Freedom is also a state of non-doing whether mentally or physically. This state comes closest to what we call Infinite Intelligence – an originator and sustainer of our universe and beyond. Yet, Infinite Intelligence' "non-doing" means doing absolutely everything but in ways yet inconceivable.

Unlike Infinite Intelligence, being in a state of Freedom we cannot originate or create anything. We can only experience the unencumbered peace that entirely transforms our being so that when we "step down" or come back to the dreamland we are able to think, imagine and create while being led by Love, which is the same state that we experience as the result of the *transformation*.

A simple and persistent reminder could do a great deal of work if not magic. As you move through your day, turn your every thought into a loving thought, every feeling – into a loving feeling. As you do this, you will be elevated into the world of Love. Do not get discouraged if in the beginning, you may forget to follow this route. Gently remind yourself to continue and keep enjoying it. When you get irritated or annoyed, instantly remind yourself of Love, smile and you are back on track, feeling loving again. To ensure the success of this practice you would need to learn to watch your mind (explained below) and to love yourself.

The Lie of Principle adopted from *The Lion Moves Alone*

When we do not have confidence in Love, in what is real, what is natural, we live by the principles. We live by what we have been taught by parents, teachers, society, and religion. We have been taught to believe in principles.

A reader was complaining: "No one wants to be a friend with a guillotine." He is right: except for gravediggers, no one wants to handle corpses. He turned himself into a guillotine. His principle is to cut off the heads to all those who are not in agreement with his principles. This means cutting off many heads. Yet, to him, it does not matter. What matters is a principle. He is 50, and he will live another 70 years. Does it make any sense? He is already dead: a guillotine, a piece of metal.

When we are not aware, we are nearly dead; we are existing mechanically, existing with habits and dead principles. It cannot be otherwise because when awareness is low, principle becomes a ruler whether it is guillotine or kindness. If you are greedy, you could try to make yourself a kind person and kindness will become your principle but you will not become kindness. You would remain the same person but now your greed will be covered with a mask of kindness. Only when Love is realized you will become kindness and Love.

Misha landed in the US several years back. A year later, he invited his young daughter Masha and she decided to stay in America. Soon, Masha became a quite successful young woman but her relationship with father deteriorated. The two were close to me and I was trying to have them talk, yet father refused to talk to his daughter because he wanted to be true to his principle: "When people betray me I cut them off forever, whether they are friends, children or relatives." Masha did not betray her father. There was unpleasant arguing a couple of times. After that, neither father nor daughter wanted to make the first call. Father said he is indifferent to his daughter. Yet, there is no such thing as indifference, which is simply a cover for negative emotions (sadness and frustration in this case) we do not wish to face.

Society and religion cultivate inferior people by making them adopt principles. Both religion and society are satisfied: these people are easier to rule. The Holy Inquisition of the Catholic Church that for 800 years was burning people alive in the name of loving God is a good example of how principle turns human beings into monsters. Roman popes had rarely attended these holy fires. The 'unfaithful', their children and wives have been burned alive by those who lived by the principles of the holy church, created by the ignorant men.

In school, we have been told of importance abiding the principles. We were taught supreme principles. Unfortunately, being an artificial creation of unaware minds, even supreme principles are a dead weight. Make a note of how society describes this tool of control:

The principle is 1. The fundamental truth, law, a moving force that creates the basis for other truths, laws and moving forces. 2. A governing condition, main rule, the directive for any kind of action. 3. Inner conviction, the point of view, the standard of behavior.

Principles are created by the desire to be right, by the desire to assert. At the core of violence, there is always a principle that justifies it. Nothing exposes the nature of a principle better than its endeavor to justify violence. Principles are never truthful. There are many seem to be useful principles in a dreamland. However, none of these principles will help you to wake up and move beyond the illusion of dreamland. Society lives by its principles but in nature, in the flow of Life there is no need for principles, and people are an integral part of nature.

When living in the present, when you realize Love you can live in the society and be beyond its principles. Someone may say true Love is also a principle. It is true but only for the one who talks about Love; when one has realized Love, there is no more principles but a peaceful state of Love.

In the dreamland, the principle is made important. To the one who walks the road of Love and Freedom there are no useful principles because every principle is a limitation. In the world of Love, belief and faith are but empty words.

Love and Freedom are unprincipled. Honesty and kindness are our nature. Ignorance manipulates principles; it divides by principles. It creates enemies with principles. 'Who is not with us, is against us.' If there were no enemy, this principle certainly will help to create one. Even like the selfish desire that is not rooted in Love, the principle is an impediment on the way to Happiness; it undermines Love, for any principle is but a selfish desire.

Buddha was unprincipled; his followers created 32 schools of Buddhism. You may wonder why. There was one Buddha with a simple teaching, now there are 32 teachings, and a new religion called Buddhism. They did it to prove that "my principle" is the right principle. Buddha was unprincipled, but the followers created 32 new principles. Jesus was teaching Love. Like Buddha, Jesus was unprincipled. Like any other enlightened teacher, Jesus created no school, no organization, but the followers were ignorant. The followers created the whole system of principles called Christian Religion.

It has happened so many times throughout history: unprincipled enlightened teacher dies, principled ignorant followers create new religion… and millenniums of suffering. When a selfish desire is at the root of creation the result is smeared with suffering but when there is a canning desire, the result is disastrous. To protect itself, ignorance builds prison bars of principles through which no Love can shine. Religion has manufactured its artificial world with rigid dogmatic principles – the same prison bars. Love is Life that carries everything in its stream, including religion. Ignorance fears Love because when is exposed to the light of Love, ignorance evaporates.

Resistance

Peter came to Moscow from Germany, looking for new business opportunities. Instead, he fell in Love with 28-year-old Natasha. Several months later Peter went back to Germany and Natasha gave birth to a little girl Masha. When Masha was one month old, Peter invited Natasha and their little daughter to Munich.

Yet, when arrived to the Munich airport, Natasha was up for a great shock. A little man came up to her, introduced himself as Peter's friend and said that Peter did not come because he has just got married.

That shock was never transformed into Love but kept influencing Natasha for the rest of her life. Peter passed away 10 years into past. Now, at over 60, Natasha (her conscious mind) believes that shock is a long-forgotten thing, that she does not care about it any longer, that she never things about Peter and when it happens she is only thankful to Peter for gifting hr with Masha....

Yet, when Peter passed away, Masha casually mentioned "There was some disturbance... Peter passed away... otherwise everything is fine." Not only Natasha's subconscious kept remembering that terrible shock all this time... that shock's negativity was also transferred to Masha. It helped to form Masha's negative attitude towards her father.

A child – parent relationship is of a very sensitive nature. Even when the child does not remember one or both parents, he or she will think about them often throughout life. This is harmless. Yet, when parents did something wrong, that negativity will influence the child's life whether it is remembered by the child's conscious mind or not, for subconscious forgets nothing. The negativity, whether remembered or hidden in the subconscious can be eliminated only with *transformation.*

"...But honestly, I can't say I love my parents 100%. There are some remains of rage, hate, and fear. My family's was a dramatic story, the story that is still alive in my mind after all these years. It is difficult to love people who destroyed almost everything they had for not being able to forgive each other. The hardest part is that of my mother who was daily killing herself from the age of 40 years on, with drinking, smoking 40 cigarettes a day, lying in bed watching TV and never caring for her health, her children or the house. I need to release all that. But please can you explain again to me why you said that releasing only can't take you to the deeper subconscious and the methods you use to get there?"

This letter is an example of the powerful resistance program and conditioning that often are barring people from understanding this chapter. *Transformation* is a quite simple process. What makes it look complicated is resistance and conditioning – the mind's limitations that are justifying and guarding our ignorance.

...releasing cannot take you to the deeper subconscious for several reasons. Releasing remains in the realm of the limited mind while realized Love takes us beyond mind's limitations. Releasing is a man-created concept; thus, it cannot be without limitations while Love is our essence; it is free from limitations. In itself, releasing has no power while realized Love is the most powerful force in the human world. With every negative situation transformed into Love, we gradually begin to use this force. Our full possession of this force comes with the realization of Love.

- Learn how to watch you mind (explained below) so that you effortlessly know what is in there at every moment.

- Learn to love yourself unconditionally, regardless of the negativity you may presently harbor. You accumulated it you can transform it. Giving yourself plenty of approval as often as possible is a wonderful way to start falling in love with yourself.

- Make irrevocable decision to transform your past into Love, regardless of what you presently feel about *transformation*.

- This chapter has everything you need to begin transforming your past into Love. You may find it useful to do some adjustments. Be creative.

- Read this chapter carefully again and again until you feel comfortable with it.

-Resistance is usually expressed in laziness, procrastination, and unwillingness to do what needs to be done. It will trick you into asking questions. Asking questions is resistance's way postponing what needs to be done. Do not fall into this trap. Try to get answers from within. Allow yourself to ask questions only after you failed to get them from within. Transform resistance into Love to your mind and move on with the process.

It is our impatience and the lack of trust in our Self – Love that blocks the answers from coming. If you didn't get the answer from within, let the question in question stay in the back of yore mind. Be patient and utterly convinced the answer will service. Be expectant like a pregnant woman is expectant of giving birth to a healthy baby.

- Do not philosophize, discuss, judge or criticize events and emotions you are transforming. Just witness it and transform…

Start practicing even if you have some unanswered questions. Trust yourself. In the process, most questions will lose their importance; others will be answered. Keep practicing and like Lester, you may be able to enhance the process with your own approach while using hints and suggestions given in this book.

Lester understood that he could change into Love past negative events using logic, common sense and... *something intuitive inexplicable else*.... It is because of this *something inexplicable individual else* that the limited mind is trying to compromise *transformation*: the mind that was leading you to problems and mistakes cannot understand what is beyond its limitations. Yet, with perseverance, you will discover this *something inexplicable individual else*. It may or may not be expressed in words. It may be a hint you get at doing something right in a particular situation... Most likely, it will be an intuitive discovery. You would "feel" it as encouragement, as assurance of success. You will discover it sooner when at the very beginning of the practice you will choose Love to be your guide.

Do not get discouraged with initial failures. It took Lester some time to get results. We are in an incomparably better position than Lester was because we have a proven method while Lester was searching in the dark. You have the light of the right knowledge. Just do it! Transform into Love one particular situation. Stay with it, finish it then move to another event.

It may be even not a specific feeling of hate, anger or fear that you would be dealing with, it could be a welter of negativity that my friend (in the above example) convinced himself he had the right to feel. Yet, if he has thus convinced himself, he also can convince himself of the opposite.

Conditioning and resistance, which are part of the ego or ignorance, are standing guard against Love because the realization of Love means the death of the ego. Ego means judgment: *My family's was a dramatic story, the story that is still alive in my mind after all these years. It is difficult to love people who destroyed almost everything they had for not being able to forgive each other.* On the surface, it sounds right but only on the surface because we have neither right no need to judge, criticize or try to change someone's behavior. Love will never do that. The only ego believes it has right to barge into someone else's life whenever it wants.

However, when said from Love's point of view, the sentence will change because *Love's point of view* means the absence of the ego. When there is no ego, there is no judgment but compassionate witnessing. Not colored with emotions, a witness sees and speaks out the truth without being influenced by what is seen and said. When the above sentence is spoken from *Love's point of view* it would reflect compassion, understanding, and acceptance: *Sadly, my parents destroyed their lives because they were not able to forgive each other.*

An ignorant mind may not want to give up negative emotions because there may be something masochistically "good" about keeping them in: a bitter sweetness in experiencing their pain again and again. Keep on going and transform this bitter sweetness into Love.

The answer my friend is seeking may be hidden in his own letter, in this spontaneously written line: "It is difficult to love people who destroyed almost everything they had <u>for not being able to forgive</u> each other." Have you been able to forgive your parents? Forgiveness is compassion and understanding, which is Love.

You need to succeed only once and the rest of the process will be easy, enjoyable.

True wisdom seems foolish to the ignorant mind. Because people do not believe in the power and magic of Love, a cultural conditioning takes over and creates obstacles in their way. The most dominant of these obstacles is Resistance. This program is guarding negativity as well as all other subconscious programs. Consequently, the mind resists/rejects anything that is not in accordance with concepts accepted by it as truthful.

The mind's stronghold Resistance program can be compared with an impregnable wall. Unless rooted in Love our every experience and concept becomes a brick that reinforces this wall, cemented with ignorance. As we live, this wall of Resistance grows thicker and higher. The Resistance program is but our past; it is so powerful because it becomes an integral part of our subconscious. This is why most people are either ignoring Love and *transformation* altogether or giving it up after just a few attempts. "Don't bother," the mind brags, "you're wasting your time," and a person quickly agrees: "Yeah, it is not for me, I have to find something else." Yet, there is no "something else" that is as powerful and effective as *transformation*, except meditation, which would require more time.

Resistance is deeply embedded and cannot be released, destroyed, dissolved or otherwise eliminated. Yet, when we *transform* our past into Love, the Resistance program becomes obsolete because Love neither fights nor resists, it elevates us into a higher realm of Love where we understand and accept.

In his book, *Thus Spake Zarathustra* Friedrich Nietzsche (who was purposefully misinterpreted by the Nazis and is misunderstood even today) speaks of the three human states of Camel, Lion, and Child. The Camel is lazy and dull; its Resistance program is all-powerful. The next higher state is Lion. When we realize we have been missing life while idling with crowds or in front of the idiot box, we begin to move up and out in our search for truth, and we roar. Our Resistance program is still strong, but it is weakening. With *transformation,* we transcend all resistance. When *transformation* process is completed, the "wall" of resistance is left in a dreamland and the child emerges in the state of Love, an innocent, spontaneous and loving child with adult experience.

Whatever state you are presently in, it will evolve, but only when you are determined to grow into a life of Happiness and Success. If you are already successful, your success most likely is not fulfilling. The reason is your negative past, the "sorry scheme of things" you created unaware. Now being aware, re-mold your life into a life of your heart's desire.

Indeed, true Love is threatening the mind's supremacy. The limited mind is very suspicious of Love because it cannot understand it. The mind's Resistance program is on and running, for until your past is transformed, the mind would not embrace Love. In its present state mind cannot know that it will enjoy its new position of a loving loyal servant.

Until our past is *transformed,* the mind will continue to dominate and try to make decisions often solely on its own. Yet, you can ask Love for advice on every matter.

Resistance can make it hard for you to accept someone you do not like but it cannot prevent you from asking Love for advice. Love's guidance will temporarily take you beyond resistance because Love knows neither resistance nor other limitations created by the mind. When you use it, it is inexhaustible. Decide for Love to be your guide and taste the power of Love.

The limited mind is very tricky, and it makes mistakes. Resistance is the mind's weapon, which it uses constantly, especially when something is threatening its supremacy. Yet, all the mind's weapons are powerless against Love's guidance. Love's guidance will be of a great help in your *transformation* process.

Love is never mistaken. However, until Love is realized the mind is still in charge; it will make you doubt Love's advice and push for its own solution. Until your past is transformed into love, you may still follow your mind's advice... Yet, it is good to have a choice and in the end, you will realize that Love is always right. When you need to make a decision, immediately, the mind will come up with suggestions. Listen to it, then relax, bring yourself into a more loving state and then ask for Love's advice on the same matter. You will be pleasantly surprised with what you get.

Appreciation and gratitude both are properties of Love. In every situation of your past and no matter how complex it was, find something or someone to be thankful and appreciative for. This also will help derail your Resistance program for a while.

Gratitude… there is a wonderful Japanese story (adapted here from Zenkei Shibayama Roshi's *A Flower Does Not Talk*) which portrays this feeling:

A hundred and fifty years ago, there lived a woman named Sono whose purity of heart was respected far and wide. One day a fellow-Buddhist, having made a long trip to see her, asked, "What can I do to put my heart at rest?" She said, "Every morning and every evening, and whenever anything happens to you keep saying, "Thanks for everything. I have no complaint whatsoever." The man did as he was instructed for a whole year but his heart still was not at peace. He returned to Sono crestfallen "I've said your prayer over and over and yet nothing in my life has changed; I am still the same selfish person as before. What should I do now?" Sono immediately said, "Thanks for everything. I have no complaint whatsoever." On hearing that the man was able to awake and return home with a great joy.

Still, some other helpful points are, *start small* and learn how to *enjoy every instant.* To help deal with resistance, start small and enjoy each instant of the process, regardless of having difficulties. For example, meditation is as much a threat to the mind's supremacy as *transformation*, if not more... As soon as I learned of meditation, I decided to start meditating 15-minute sessions. Instantly, my Resistance program kicked in. The mind reminded me of the tasks to be accomplished at once, saying that I can meditate afterward. I was about to obey it but realized that my mind simply had tricked me, for the tasks could surely wait for another 15 minutes.

I sat down determined not to move a muscle for at least 15 minutes and... failed. Yet, I was able to watch my mind uninterrupted for about twenty or thirty seconds. Learning from the experience, I made my next session only three minutes long. It took me several days to accomplish this small task. Yet, in less than six months of gradually increasing sessions, I was able to meditate one hour.

In the beginning, do not try to love someone you hate. Instead, go back to your early childhood memories and start with *transforming* into Love your earliest hurts. Let Love to guide you, use logic and common sense. Some negative memories are much stronger than the others are. Start with those that are easier to deal with and remind yourself to enjoy every moment of the process.

My friend's girlfriend had a disastrous relationship experience. It was all over about two years in the past yet, she does not suspect how badly that experience is influencing her present relationship. "I don't think about him anymore," She said, "I have no feelings for him." With her permission, I explained to her the essence of *transformation*. At once, I realized it was the wrong start. Tears ran from her eyes and she exclaimed in an utter disdain, "To love him!" She turned away, sobbing. Her subconscious kept "thinking" about him despite her trying to convince herself otherwise. Two years after that relationship ended, just a reminder of that man was too much for her. Yet, later she became curious and started practicing *transformation* but only a year later.

We can bury our hurts deep inside, so deep we do not even think about it. Yet, it will keep working against us from the subconscious underground, silently sabotaging our relationships and goals.

I wrote about Jerry and Fritzie's 65-year-long relationship in *Freedom Technique: Path to Awareness and Love*. It was truly exceptional. Yet, Jerry and Fritzie are also a good example of the conditioning, which they inflicted upon themselves. Communism is a very appealing concept, but it is not executable because the masses' awareness is still low. Accepting this concept as doable Jerry and Fritzie joined Canadian Communist Party at a very young age. In the sixties, they had learned about Soviet concentration camps and psychiatric prisons but did not give up their belief in the Soviet communism.

When 20 years later I asked them why they are so convinced in a concept that is proven time and time again to be wrong, Fritzie replied, "We are too old to change." Age is not an obstacle but when we are knowingly harboring some negativity, we have to justify it at least to ourselves. This inevitably creates an inner conflict, which is quietly disturbing.

The mind may adopt concepts of communism and democracy as truthful but Love accepts and understands what these concepts are. It is much more practical to adopt no concepts because any concept is just another limitation. With Love, we would accept all concepts but only for the people who created and adopted them. As to ourselves, we would not adopt any concept.

To reiterate… "I've forgotten about it a long time ago…" No, you did not; your subconscious forgets nothing. "Time heals" Wrong again. Only Love can heal your negative experiences. Every such excuse is just another trick of the mind caused by the resistance and conditioning – an attempt to escape the truth.

In my meditation experience, the key was not only in starting small but also in learning how to enjoy every moment, regardless of failures. It was very hard to sit in a meditating posture. In the beginning, it was almost a torturous experience. Yet, almost like a masochist, I made myself to enjoy the posture. It helped and within a few months, the posture seized to be a problem.

The enjoyment helps in many ways, including an instant disabling Resistance program. It also makes your work more effective and pleasant. When you are done with *transformation*, you will be effortlessly enjoying every moment but in the beginning of the process, you will often need to remind yourself of the enjoyment. Truly, why not to enjoy each moment of the *transformation*? It is so natural to enjoy each instance of our growth, for when transformed into Love, every past situation moves us closer to the state of Love.

Moments of negativity are harmful. A moment of life not enjoyed is the moment lost. Life is short no matter how many years one lives. We must enjoy each instant; there should be no excuses. This will become obvious to you at some point in the *transformation* process. In the course of practice, you will become more loving, more often and naturally guided by Love, and joy will happen naturally. You will also become a witness to the process. Though true witnessing seems to be impartial, it is rooted in Love.

Conditioning

Conditioning is a process used by individuals, society, government, religion, etc. to train, tame and otherwise habituate human mind with certain ideas, concepts, and ideology. There are numberless ways and methods used by various entities to condition the human mind: government, corporate and religious propaganda, advertising, special interest groups' ideology and educational conditioning used in various learning institutions, social media, etc., Conditioning means slavery. Realization of Love ends slavery.

For one who does not realize Love, it is impossible to withstand today's flow of conditioning. When affected by this flood, which is often a misinformation, people get confused, disoriented. They cannot distinguish true journalism from fake news and fall victim to fear, uncertainty and insecurity.

When words "fake news" are entered in a search engine, it may identify fake news sites, yet, it is not these sites but the entire organization of elite media is fake news. Speeches of the presidents and lawmakers are fake news; analyses and discussions broadcast by the media are mostly fake news.

When the mind is conditioned with a negative concept like Fascism, it becomes corrupted and self-distracted. It is the same with a concept which seems to be good such as of communism. When the mind is conditioned by some ideology whether it is good as democracy or bad as fascism, it becomes utterly resistant to any other ideological concept, it does not want to hear about Love. Religious conditioning separates people and nations.

The military that turns a human being into a heartless robot is a graphic demonstration of the most harmful conditioning. Consequences of the conditioning by the military are tragic as it creates brutal, psychologically unstable humans.

A mind conditioned is a mind controlled. This control is effectively exercised from without. We cannot control the mind with conditioning. Only with Love we can exercise natural, effortless and beneficial mind control.

I love this quote as it also is suggesting how one can effectively avoid conditioning:

Believe not because some old manuscripts are produced, believe not because it is your national belief, believe not because you have been made to believe from your childhood, but reason truth out, and after you have analyzed it, then if you find it will do good to one and all, believe it, live up to it and help others live up to it.

Whatever concept you are about to accept, drop it unless it conforms this quote, for Buddha speaks here of true Love. Adopt only concepts that measure up to Love… yet, there are no such concepts☺ because every concept whether negative or positive will not measure up to Love but limit it. Any concept can be understood and accepted for the sake of the concept and/or people behind it, but it must not be adopted. When not adopted, a concept will not influence you. It will become a piece of information that you may either use or discard. Adopting means accepting a concept as being true, which will log it into the subconscious.

Every concept is contributing to conditioning. Love is beyond all concepts and beyond conditioning. If you are employing a mantra or an affirmation, unless it is rooted in Love, it is not for your benefit. When an affirmation is rooted in Love, it will measure up to the above quote. You may check any of your concepts against this quote and learn that all of them could be discarded for only Love *is* most effective at *doing good to one and all*.

Conditioning and resistance are reinforcing each other. Depending on the kind of conditioning, as soon as it becomes a part of ourselves, it can also be deadly. The

Realization of Love eliminates both conditioning and resistance. If you are selfish, you may try to condition yourself into being kind with affirmations, logic and common sense. You may also use releasing... However, you can achieve a permanent state of kindness only with *transformation*.

In another example, our society is conditioning people to a belief that democracy is real in this country. Yet, a true democracy cannot coexist with inequality. When there is an inequality, the democracy is true only for the rich.

Buddha's saying is but a tribute to Love as well as it is a warning of the conditioning. Are you an individuality or a personality, which is individuality conditioned by the philosophies, religion, teachings, concepts, etc., – a lost individuality? Transform all acquired dross into Love and discover anew your open and loving individuality.

The impact of the social groups' conditioning could help explain why religion might in a very literal sense be what Karl Marx defined as "the opium of the people": it can condition us into believing its dogma and God, into it being the best religion to follow, into criticizing, even despising other religions and those who follow them. A conditioning becomes more effective when we are in the crowd of other believers.

Stay away from crowds.

This summer I will publish an unusual and beautiful love story titled *The 41st*. This true story demonstrates with unparalleled vividness a deadly impact of the ideological/cultural conditioning on the human mind. At all times, one's awareness is in a direct proportion with a degree of the conditioning. The more your subconscious and the conscious mind is conditioned/clogged with information related to life, whether negative or positive, the less you are aware.

When conditioning is predominantly negative awareness falls to its lowest, as in the case of Fascist Germany, USSR or Mao's China where countless millions were killed by their compatriots conditioned with the murderous ideology.

In personal relationships, in the beginning, conditioning that has been deeply embedded into the subconscious may be temporarily overridden by the excitement of a new relationship. Yet, the subconscious never "forgets" its conditioning and will strike a blow to its owner at a time least expected.

It is the same with business relations and decisions: when there is no Love, our subconscious is in charge and is silently influencing everything we do. It is not conscious mind but subconscious that makes people so different from one another. Subconscious is ruling the mind. However, when Love is realized, Love becomes our only ruler. Unlike the mind influenced by the subconscious, Love is influenced by nothing and is mistake-proof.

Witnessing the mind

When you wish to improve your life, watching the mind is a must.

The resistance of the *transformation* is the resistance of the acceptance of Love as our guide. The mind has been our guide for such a long time… it made us subjects to itself. The mind does not want to give up control for it trusts nothing but itself. The mind resists choosing Love's guidance because of our thinking habit: we love to think, but also hate it when mind keeps thinking on its own and we cannot control it. Love, on the other hand, does not think but communicate its message via intuition, which is another enigma to the limited mind.

In many people's Love was blocked in their childhood – covered with negativity much of which has been chosen under the pretense of being necessary for survival. At the same time, the resistance program was created – a safeguard of the negative conditioning.

Though most people understand that Love is important, they are not guided by Love because the mind accepts Love only on the surface and on its own terms, which is "I love this person but I hate that one." As Love is beyond the mind's conditioning the mind can neither understand (true) Love's absolute importance for a life of Happiness. When the mind is educated, it will understand and begin to co-operate with *transformation*. Yet, even when co-operating, the mind will often try to subvert *transformation*. Educate your mind with the *right knowledge* and teach it how to watch itself.

Just watch the mind without reacting to your thoughts, as if you are witnessing someone else's mind or as you are watching a train pass by. There is nothing complicated about it. Just consistently remind yourself to watch the mind until witnessing becomes as effortless as breathing. By this time, you will know your mind well and the gaps of quiet in between your thoughts will increase.

With practice, the mind will begin to watch itself without effort on your part. At that time, you will be able effortlessly and instantly to let go/transform into Love any negative thought and emotion. That is how simple it is: decision and watching, watching, and watching, that is all.

Learning how to watch the mind may be likened to learning how to ride a bicycle. Until we begin to practice, it seems very difficult to ride on two wheels. Once we learned how to ride, it becomes natural; we do not ever think about it again. It is the same with witnessing the mind ☺ At first, it seems a strange and difficult thing to do. Yet, as you begin practicing the ease and benefits of the witnessing become manifest.

The mind is naturally empty and only when it remains empty, without grasping and rejecting, can it respond to natural things without prejudice. It should be like a river gorge with swan flying overhead. The river has no desire to retain the swan; yet, the swan's passing is traced by its shadow without any omission. Another example: a mirror will reflect things perfectly, whether they are beautiful or ugly. It never refuses to show a thing, no does it retain the thing after it is gone. The mind should be as open as this.
Ling-Ching-hsi

*The mind opens naturally w*ith the realization of Love.

Become your own best teacher

> Oh, come with old Khayyam, and leave the wise
> To talk; one thing is certain that life flies;
> One thing is certain, and the rest is lies;
> The flower that once has blown forever dies.

What is life's purpose if not a true Happiness? When you make an irrevocable decision for a life of Happiness to be your purpose, also decide to become your own teacher.

Most people on the path spend much time searching, attending seminars, and studying teachings… This is the natural learning process. However, to everything there is a season and the time for every purpose under heaven. You have done much research and studying… and you do not want to spend your life doing it over and over again. You want the results now and you can have them.

By now, you probably learn that true answers could come only from within and this would happen only when you will become your own teacher.

Really, you have no choice because you already are your own best teacher with all the knowledge available to you. The question is how to access it, and the answer is Love. Love is all you need to access the necessary information, for Love is but the secret valve that opens the flow of intuition carrying the information you need at any given moment. It is only with Love that you will find all you need.

For millenniums, the wise have been affirming that every human being is his own best teacher. It is even more so today with much information freely available. Lester said much about Love, Happiness, and Freedom. Andrew Carnegie provided an enlightening example of Love's infinite power.

We have Lester, a true Master of our time and a proven method of *transformation*. We have Carnegie's example where Love helped to create the greatest business success of all time. We also have a present-day example of *The Giving People* and numerous examples of the people led by Love. We have everything necessary to become our own best teachers.

Is there any other state of being which is greater than Love bordering with peace of Freedom? With Love, you recognize your talent, employ it and achieve Success. With Love, you find Happiness. As you complete transforming your past, you will find yourself at the "border". Beyond this border is Freedom. At that moment, you may be subtly persuaded to move on, which is a definite sign of your ability to find Freedom.

A small window of time
That's all we are
A brilliant sunrise
A falling star

The burst of orange
The morning sky
Just a moment
Before heaven's cry

The setting sun
Its final show
Takes our breath away
As we see it go

A small window of time
From birth to death
A sacred gift
From breath to breath

Lifting the shade
Won't cost a dime
For a priceless view
From the window of time

David Kettler

The Needles. Sequoia National Forest, Southern California

True dreamers of the American dream

George Washington, who often felt he was being guided by Love, said in his "Farewell Address":

"It will be worthy of a free, and enlightened, and at no distant period a great, nation to give to mankind the magnanimous and too novel example of a people always guided by an exalted justice and benevolence. Who can doubt that, in the course of time and things, the fruits of such a plan would richly repay any temporary advantages, which might be lost by a steady adherence to it? Can it be that Providence has not connected the permanent felicity of a nation with its virtue?"

Andrew Carnegie was guided by Love and *benevolence*. *The Gospel of Wealth* was published in the beginning of the last century. Carnegie believed the rich would follow in his steps; he was mistaken only in timing.

Today, as if celebrating a 100 anniversary of *The Gospel of Wealth* the *True Dreamers of the American Dream* are pledging their fortunes to the improvement of the people's well-being in the US and around the world. Indeed, *The Giving People* are being guided by Love, *an exalted justice, and benevolence*. Every member of this forum publicly pledged a major portion of wealth with some givers dedicating their entire assets to charitable causes.

Following are remarkable excerpts from the pledges. You will find complete pledges at TheGivingPeople.com. Every pledge is a revelation where you may discover sound ideas. You would learn that every member of *The Giving People* initiative is led by understanding, acceptance, and compassion. A loving upbringing has been a major factor in shaping most of these people's personalities.

"In 2006, I made a commitment to gradually give all my Berkshire Hathaway stock to philanthropic foundations. I could not be happier with that decision. Now, Bill and Melinda Gates and I are asking hundreds of rich Americans to pledge at least 50% of their wealth to charity." So, I think it is fitting that I reiterate my intentions and explain the thinking that lies behind them...

"...The reaction of my family and me to our extraordinary good fortune is not guilt, but rather a gratitude. Were we to use more than 1% of my claim checks on ourselves, neither our happiness nor well-being would be enhanced. In contrast, that remaining 99% can have a huge effect on the health and welfare of others. That reality sets an obvious course for me and my family: Keep all we can conceivably need and distribute the rest to society, for its needs. My pledge starts us down that course."

Warren Buffett

"...Our animating principle is that all lives have equal value. Put another way, it means that we believe every child deserves the chance to grow up, to dream and do big things. We have been blessed with good fortune beyond our wildest expectations, and we are profoundly grateful. But just as these gifts are great, so we feel a great responsibility to use them well. That is why we are so pleased to join in making an explicit commitment to the Giving Pledge."

Bill & Melinda Gates

"...My earliest memories include my father's exhortations about how important it is to give back. These early teachings were ingrained in me, and a portion of the first dollars I earned, I gave away. Over the years, the emotional and psychological returns I have earned from charitable giving have been enormous. The more I do for others, the happier I am. The happiness and optimism I have obtained from helping others are a big part of what keeps me sane."

Bill and Karen Ackman

"It is with a profound sense of relief that I am able to write this letter, expressing my intent to give away the vast majority of my wealth. Having the opportunity to help others achieve a better and more fulfilling life is not only an enormous privilege but also a lifelong dream. Several years ago, I received the support of my two young daughters, Jane and Hilary, in this pursuit. At an early age, my daughter, Jane, encouraged me to devote all of my resources to philanthropy and my dream of helping others. She assured me that my love and happiness were far more important to her than any inheritance she might receive."

Sue Ann Arnall

"About a decade ago I made a decision based on a destiny that had been defined 42 years previously. That decision was to start focusing much more on helping others in desperate need, rather than focusing on my own wealth creation. For this reason, along with the influence of other catalysts, I decided to sell my business, which I eventually did in 2006.

"About the same time, I decided that I was going to give at least half my wealth away when I died, as well as trying to change as many lives as possible during my lifetime. Part of this decision process was that I really don't think it is healthy and desirable for children to have such vast amounts of wealth left to them, and my philosophy is very much to encourage my children to forge their own success and happiness, even though that will undoubtedly involve much more modest levels of wealth creation."

John Caudwell

"Being a first generation American has many rewards. Among them is having the opportunity to succeed in this free country, and then succeeding enough to have the privilege of knowing that "success unshared is a failure." My mother raised my brother and me in a European immigrant community in downtown Los Angeles. From the time I was two years old, it was just the three of us. We didn't have very much, not even a TV; however, we did not realize that.

"One Christmas, when I was six years old, my mother took us to see the window displays and decorations in the big department stores in downtown Los Angeles. It was a big treat for us. We saw puppets that moved and trains that circled... It was really special and added to the Christmas spirit, but it didn't cost anything. That same year, my mother gave my brother and me a dime. She told both of us to hold half of it and put it in the bucket near a man who was ringing a bell. We did, and then we asked my mother why we gave him the dime (at the time, a dime could buy you three candy bars or two soda pops).

"My mom's reply was, "This is the Salvation Army that helps people who are really in need. Remember boys, no matter how much you have, there is always someone who is more in need than you. Always try to give, even if it is a little." Needless to say, that stuck with me in my adult life. Now my family and I have the privilege to help people and make the world a better place to live. This opportunity will not be passed up.

"Living is giving. I won't deprive my family of knowing how good it feels to help those in need with some of the basics we already have…food, shelter, care and a future. Whether it's feeding thousands of orphans in third world countries, saving whales, helping the homeless find employment, protecting our waterways, rescuing young girls from prostitution, teaching and supplying families in Appalachia with equipment to grow their own vegetables or any other worthwhile endeavor…giving back is a practice and joy I want my family to continue. I plan to help the world now and in the future — through my trust and my family — with half (if not more) of what I have been blessed with today. Peace, love and happiness: John Paul DeJoria Co-Founder John Paul Mitchell Systems Co-Founder Patron Spirits Company Co-Founder John Paul Pet Co-Founder ROK"

John Paul DeJoria

"The work of my life has been to develop software that would help keep people well and help sick people get better. It's been to create a system that allows us to discover the dangers of drugs like Thalidomide or Chloromycetin earlier before kids are harmed. It's to enable studies of data that bring us cures for cancer and resolve autism. It's to share information with other healthcare organizations wherever the patient goes.

Many years ago I asked my young children what two things they needed from their parents. They said 'food and money.' I told them 'roots and wings.' My goal in pledging 99% of my assets to philanthropy is to help others with roots—food, warmth, shelter, healthcare, education—so they too can have wings."

Judith R. Faulkner

"There is nothing more satisfying and exciting than being able to positively affect people and noble causes in this world. We are fortunate to be in the position to join the Giving Pledge and state publicly that the majority of our wealth will be contributed to philanthropy during our lifetimes or after we leave this world.

This was an easy decision for us. We have both been involved with non-profit causes for many years."

Dan and Jennifer Gilbert

"From a young age, my brothers and I were taught to give to those less fortunate than ourselves, no matter how little we had. That ethos has remained at the core of our family since childhood and, today, thanks to my business success, I am very fortunate to be able to help many thousands of women and children in Africa. It is so important that those of us who have enjoyed fortune in business utilize our skills and knowledge in philanthropy to empower people to help themselves. Through my Foundations, I hope to continue to contribute to improving the lives of women and children for many years to come and I am honored to join the Giving Pledge."

Ann Gloag OBE

"My Charitable Giving Plan. It has been clear to me since my earliest childhood memories that my reason for being was to help others. The desire to give back was the impetus for pursuing an education in business, for applying that education to founding what became a successful container company, and for using that experience to grow our differentiated chemicals corporation into the global enterprise it has become. The journey which began in poverty somehow led to my name's inclusion on the Richest Americans list for several years running."

John and Karen Huntsman

"I suppose I arrived at my charitable commitment largely through guilt. I recognized early on, that my good fortune was not due to superior personal character or initiative so much as it was to dumb luck. I was blessed to be born in an advanced society with caring parents. So, I had the advantage of both genetics (winning the "ovarian lottery") and upbringing.

"As I looked around at those who did not have these advantages, it became clear to me that I had a moral obligation to direct my resources to help right that balance. America's "social contract" is equal opportunity. It is the most fundamental principle in our founding documents and it is what originally distinguished us from the old Europe. Yet, we have failed in achieving that seminal goal; in fact, we have lost ground in recent years.

"Another distinctly American principle is a shared partnership between the public and private sectors to foster the public good. So, if the democratically-directed public sector is shirking, to some degree, its responsibility to level the playing field, more of that role must shift to the private sector. As I addressed my charitable purposes, all of this seemed pretty clear: I was only peripherally responsible for my own good fortune; I was moral duty bound to help those left behind by the accident of birth; America's root principle was an equal opportunity but we were far from achieving it."

George B. Kaiser

"Dear Warren: I have responded affirmatively to the Giving Pledge. In fact, I have fulfilled that pledge already, having given more than half my wealth to charitable causes, primarily cancer research. I have also committed, and reaffirm here, that the balance of my estate — other than what is needed to support my wife during her lifetime — will also be given to charity. My thinking is rather simple: I learned as a young boy that sharing with others is the right thing to do, a lesson I observed from my father's willingness to share even our meager means with those less fortunate. Ever since it has never been difficult for me to continue to do the right thing. I trust your efforts in growing the ranks of those committed to the Giving Pledge will be matched by the effort to see those pledges fulfilled. Thank you for your leadership. Warmest Regards,"

Sidney Kimmel.

"Nancy and I are inspired by the leadership of the Giving Pledge. Fourteen years ago, when we set up our personal foundation and committed to giving 95% of our wealth to charitable causes either during our lifetimes or at our deaths, we never dreamed that there would be such a gathering of like-minded individuals who firmly believe in the favorable impact of giving to the world.

"Our home community in Houston. As longtime residents of this city, we have witnessed its extraordinary culture of entrepreneurship, which has enabled Houstonians of all backgrounds to improve their lives, use their talents and creativity, and pursue their dreams. In Houston, you are what you achieve. This stirs and motivates us to continue giving. The Kinder Foundation's mission is to enable our community to flourish by providing transformational gifts to projects dedicated primarily to three key areas: urban green space, education, and quality of life issues.

"Nancy and I grew up in small towns and firmly believe in the opportunity for entrepreneurship in America and especially in Houston and we believe in giving back to society the bulk of the good fortune we have received. Our goal in joining the Giving Pledge is to encourage those in similar positions to do the same."

         Rich and Nancy Kinder

"We have an opportunity and an obligation to prepare our children for the real world, for dealing with others in practical, project-based environments. It's about working together and building character — being compassionate, empathetic, and civil as a means to a greater end. As technology changes, so do students. So should classrooms, and so should our methods of teaching. In a few short years, connectivity has gone from a technological novelty to a daily necessity. It's how our culture communicates, and our children are at the forefront of its use.

"Understanding those tools — and how to integrate them into learning — is an integral step in defining our future. My pledge is to the process; as long as I have the resources at my disposal, I will seek to raise the bar for future generations of students of all ages. I am dedicating the majority of my wealth to improving education. It is the key to the survival of the human race. We have to plan for our collective future — and the first step begins with the social, emotional, and intellectual tools we provide to our children.

"As humans, our greatest tool for survival is our ability to think and to adapt — as educators, storytellers, and communicators our responsibility is to continue to do so."

George Lucas and Mellody Hobson

"I too believe that all our efforts in creating the wealth that we have would give us a great deal more joy if we were to disperse as much of it during our lifetimes. We've been focused on this work at The Marcus Foundation since our conversation many years ago. For example, The Georgia Aquarium, which is the largest in the world, has given over 12 million visitors the joy of seeing fish and mammals that the overwhelming majority would have never had the opportunity to see in their lifetime.

"It also helped stimulate our downtown economy offering jobs and new opportunities. The work we do with hospitals, education, and children through the Marcus Autism Center (MAC), has enabled us to take care of well over 36,000 children since its inception and approximately 4,000 children annually. If it weren't for the MAC in Georgia there would be nowhere for many of these families to go. I share this with you because of happiness one can conceive by watching the joys of their work."

Bernie and Billi Marcus

"Dear Warren, Bill, and Melinda, We've long embraced the principles of The Giving Pledge. Charity is something we learned at an early age, whether during grade school riding our bikes around the neighborhood collecting dimes and quarters for the American Cancer Society, or later, participating in community service programs in high school. From the time we began formal philanthropic programs in the 1970s, we've made contributions at a rate that will assure distribution of the overwhelming majority of assets during our lifetimes.

"The charitable programs we began when we were in our early 30s to advance education and progress against life-threatening diseases were later formalized with the launch of our family foundations in 1982. Our goal has been to discover and advance inventive and effective ways of helping people help themselves and those around them to lead productive and satisfying lives. We do that primarily through our work in education and medical research."

Michael and Lori Milken

"Among the Giving Pledge partners, of course, we have different circumstances and specific thinking around the motivation for joining. In my case, many years ago I formally and privately committed more than 50% of my net worth to philanthropic causes. The issue for me then was the public disclosure of the Giving Pledge. In the end, I came to the view that by openly joining other Pledge partners I might encourage others to follow. This thought makes disclosure compelling.

"One of the admirable qualities of our great country is the history and culture of helping those less fortunate. In America giving is not unusual; it is mainstream. I always thought if I were lucky enough to be in a position to help others, I would. The vast majority of Americans are this way. This is who we are. And while separate acts of generosity are generally not remarkable, taken as a whole it defines us. I never imagined not doing my part.

"I have been lucky in two significant ways. First, I had the good luck to be raised by parents who provided me with an education, good values, and love. In other words, the odds of leading a productive life were materially tilted in my favor. Second, fortune smiled on me in my work over the past thirty years. I do work hard (probably too hard), but others have worked harder and smarter with less financial success."

         Jonathan M. Nelson

"I am very pleased to pledge that I plan to contribute the substantial majority of my assets to philanthropy. I am well on my way. I do so with great pleasure. And for several reasons. My parents were Greek immigrants who came to America at age 17, with 3rd-grade education, not a word of English and hardly a penny in their pockets. Their dream was the American dream, not just for themselves but for their children as well. My father took a job no one else would take — washing dishes in a steamy caboose on the Union Pacific railroad.

"He ate and slept there and saved virtually every penny he made. He took those savings and started the inevitable Greek restaurant, open 24 hours a day for 365 days a year for 25 years. Throughout this period, he always sent money to his desperately poor family in Greece and fed countless numbers of hungry poor who came knocking on the back door of his restaurant. Above all else, he wanted to save so as to invest in his children's education.

"As I watched and learned from my father's example, I noticed how much pleasure his giving to others gave him. Indeed, today, I get much more pleasure giving money to what I consider worthwhile causes than making the money in the first place. As I checked with other philanthropists,

I found this was a very common experience. For example, I have been particularly pleased to support causes and institutions for which I have a passion and for which I contribute myself, that is my personal capital, as well as my financial capital."

        Peter G. Peterson

"We are among the converted having committed to giving all our net worth to philanthropy starting with a grant of $1.3 billion in 2006 to our spend-down Foundation. When you think about it, no other approach seems to make sense. Passing down fortunes from generation to generation can do irreparable harm. In addition, there is no way to spend a fortune. How many residences, automobiles, airplanes and other luxury items can one acquire and use?

"The Buffett/Gates initiative is likely to be a major "game changer." Their partnership and dedication and their challenge to billionaires to share their wealth with the less fortunate will undoubtedly unlock a substantial amount of funds. Congratulations! As former CEOs of a highly successful financial institution, we were rewarded monetarily beyond our wildest imagination, at the same time experiencing the emotional high associated with building a great company from scratch and winning in the competitive race."

       Herb and Marion Sandler

"I grew up in a middle-class family in Canada. My dream was to be a writer who tells stories that make a difference in the world. Along the way, when I got out of business school, I became the first full-time employee and the first President of a fledgling company with an online auction service called AuctionWeb. That company later became better known by its corporate name, eBay. When the company went public in 1998, all of a sudden I went from being in debt and living in a house with five roommates, to having hundreds of millions of dollars in the value of my eBay shares.

"Until then, I had not thought much about philanthropy. But with my newfound paper wealth, I resolved to do good things for the world with that money, in smart ways. The first thing I did, in 1999, was to start the Skoll Foundation. Today, the Skoll Foundation has become the leading organization in the world supporting social entrepreneurs to drive large-scale impact. Each year, we find innovative social entrepreneurs from around the world — people like Paul Farmer of Partners in Health or Ann Cotton of Camfed — and we support them over a multiyear period."

Jeff Skoll

"There has existed in the minds of refugees, who have been embraced by this great country, a level of gratitude for the opportunities made available to us that is somewhat analogous to a debt that we feel needs to be repaid. Some of us refer to that feeling as wanting to "give back" — I personally prefer to call it wanting to "share opportunity". And in terms of the time, energy, and money already contributed by me to replicate such an opportunity for others, my family and I have already more than fulfilled the intent of the Giving Pledge."

Tad Taube

"Giving back was instilled in me by my father at a young age. In addition to being active with Rotary and other civic organizations, my dad was also philanthropic with his own small resources. Not only did he make contributions to causes that he cared about, he also supported the tuition of two African American students at his alma mater, Millsap's College in the late 1950s. It made a big impression on me to see someone as hard-charging as my father take the time to quietly help out two young people like this."

Ted Turner

"By any possible measure, I have had an extraordinarily fortunate life (and a long one) for which I am very grateful. I couldn't be more thankful for the life I have been lucky enough to live in the best country in the world. If I didn't have ten bucks in the bank, I would still feel this way. I have been so fortunate in my professional life that I want to give it back to society in a meaningful way. So, I'm happy to sign on to the Giving Pledge, because every one of us has the opportunity — and the obligation — to make a difference by helping other people."

"Unfortunately, there remain more than 40 million people who have lost their sight needlessly and those numbers are going up at an alarming rate. Half of them are blinded by untreated cataracts. In many regions of the developing world, 60-70% of all blindness is cataract-related. In addition, there are close to two hundred million who are visually impaired by cataract disease leading unfulfilled lives. This is all happening in spite of the existence of a miracle surgery called Manual Small Incision Cataract Surgery (MSICS) which takes as little as 5 minutes to perform and costs as little as $35.

"With the encouragement of my son, Jim, we founded a not-for-profit organization called HelpMeSee. Its purpose is to promote MSICS and deliver a high fidelity simulator-based training system to train 30 thousand highly skilled MSICS specialists. We have assembled a wonderful team of medical, simulator engineering, instructional courseware designers, management, development, and financial experts. I am personally committed to validating the efficacy of high fidelity simulator training of Manual Small Incision Cataract Surgery (MSICS)."

Albert Lee Ueltschi

"I have been fortunate that I grew up in a family where charity was ingrained in us from a very early age. We were immigrants to a new country, Dubai, United Arab Emirates. Even, when my father earned a small amount, a large percentage was shared with the community we lived in, sometimes at the cost of our own comfort. To this day, our underlying philosophy remains that good giving 'pinches,' meaning that the sacrifice you make, has to be felt, else, the act remains just another financial transaction in our lives; and therein lies the appeal of the Giving Pledge to us. I was also lucky that my parents were school teachers. They always placed a great emphasis on the value of education. While perhaps I didn't live up to their expectations as a student, I saw the impact they had on people's lives. I have always believed that education is key to fixing so many of the world's greatest problems: violence, poverty, and health. It all starts with education. These two pillars of charity and education have always guided me, and out of them came the Varkey Foundation, to change lives through education around the world. We, particularly, focus on capacity building interventions for teachers and school leaders and championing their work through initiatives such as the Global Teacher Prize. Everyone deserves a great teacher. Through the Giving

Pledge, we hope to take these efforts to a greater level."

Sunny & Sherly Varkey

***

These are examples of understanding and compassion practiced and practiced by *The Giving People*, talented creators of wealth. Many millions of other talents will not create wealth even when led by Love. Nevertheless, when led by Love, every talent must result in Happiness and Success.

Could compassion and wealth sharing eliminate inequality? 50 years ago, this issue was out of the question, but today *The Giving People* are proving it is achievable. Even if only one-half of all the rich persons in America join *The Giving People* inequality will begin fading out. With 90% of all American rich joining *The Giving People* inequality will cease to exist. It is not just because of the sharing but mostly because the talented American financial minds will be forever generating ever more wealth with a major part of it supporting social needs.

Do not be misled by the government attempts to discredit this initiative with paid articles implying donation money would be better used in the government budget. The government is well known for wasteful extravagant spending on itself and its military.

"Though almost all of us grew up believing in the concept of equal opportunity, most of us simultaneously carried the unspoken and inconsistent "dirty little secret" that genetics drove much of accomplishment so that equality was not achievable."

George B. Kaiser/*The Giving people*

Genetics and talent contribute to the *accomplishment* of the financial goals. *The Giving People* also contribute to equality. *The Giving People* offered their own solution to inequality. They understand that together with the talent to create wealth comes the responsibility to share it with "the poorer brethren". It is the same solution as the one offered by Andrew Carnegie's *The Gospel of Wealth*:

This, then, is held to be the duty of the man of wealth: To set an example of modest, unostentatious living, shunning display or extravagance; to provide moderately for the legitimate wants of those dependent upon him; and, after doing so, to consider all surplus revenues which come to him simply as trust funds, which he is called upon to administer, and strictly bound as a matter of duty to administer in the manner which, in his judgment, is best calculated to produce the most beneficial results for the community – the man of wealth thus becoming the mere trustee and agent for his poorer brethren, bringing to their service his superior wisdom, experience, and ability to administer, doing for them better than they would or could do for themselves.

You may notice that *The Giving People* are rarely using the word Love in their pledges, yet their charitable decisions are motivated by the sense of responsibility, compassion, and kindness..., which is Love. They are true dreamers of the American Dream living to the fullest, for nothing is as fulfilling as opportunities created to help others.

Ancient Lake Quaroun (a view from the Sahara Desert)

Addendum

Subconscious

The moving finger writes; and, having writ,
Moves on: nor all thy piety nor wit
Shall lure it back to cancel half a line,
Nor all thy tears wash out a word of it.

Besides regulating bodily processes and instincts, the subconscious serves as an archive of the events that take place in our life as well as our every emotional experience.

The archival part of the subconscious contains everything we have learned and accepted to be true or a lie, real or false, good or bad. Many past negative events are forgotten by the conscious mind yet, the subconscious is keeping their records forever. It is this archival part of the subconscious that needs to be freed of its negative content.

Whatever your position in life at the moment, it has resulted from your subconscious' miraculous ability to exert a pull at and attract things and/or circumstances your mind has been dwelling upon. This is a general rule. Genetic information may overrule this concept. There may be other exceptions to this rule. However, opposite thoughts of doubts, fears, etc., supported by corresponding feelings, as well as long forgotten concepts contrary to your purpose would obstruct or may destroy your positive intentions. This is forever happening in an average person's mind. A chaotic ETP (Emotional Thinking Process) filled with doubts, "I can't-s", fears and regrets are continuously "downloaded" in the subconscious and create a chaotic life.

The subconscious cannot be entirely controlled, but it can be cleaned. You can learn how to control ETP and what you will program in the subconscious from now on. You will begin to gain more control as soon as you start eliminating/*transforming*/ your subconscious negativity. It is not difficult but you must make a decision – an irrevocable decision to do it and act upon it. Lack of making the decision and acting upon it creates armies of procrastinators.

Tomorrow you will also have to decide. Why not today? Tomorrow you will get neither younger no wiser. Tomorrow may never come. Then, make the decision now. When you begin removing the impediments with Love, your confidence will mature and you will be able to steer your life in the desired direction.

Time is of the essence. Life flies. You cannot afford to waste your life, for this great gift is given to us only once, unless humanity will become so advanced that by the year 3000 it will be able to raise the dead. However, that is a long time to wait for ☺ Use every instant of this wonder called life to gain Happiness and Success. The decision means an action that instantly elevates you beyond time. As soon as you make this most important decision, you kill procrastination, you are off, and flying into a life so beautiful, the words can hardly describe.

My pet The Bird

Intuition

Intuition is the voice of Love. It keeps hinting you towards the right direction but you cannot hear it because the mind never stops buzzing.

When by accident intuitive messages come through to your mind, it has a good chance to be ignored or misinterpreted. The resistance program often causes the mind to distort the intuitive message.

To be guided by Love means to be guided intuitively. Intuition is the discriminating faculty that gives us a choice of two understandings of the same matter: intuitive (Love's point of view) and the mind's suggestion. Yet, the intuitive message is always right. Perfect intuition makes one a master of the right choice. *Transformation* is the best way to develop intuition.

When guided by Love you are nearly error-proofed even before you have realized Love. Those who are not guided by Love are bound to make more mistakes, one of which is the grave mistake of loss of Happiness.

A source of all knowledge whether we call it Infinite intelligence, the mind's unknown 95%, collective subconscious field or by any other name, is forever open to us via intuition. It could be even more than one source of knowledge. We do not know how intuition is accessing the source. Nevertheless, we continue to receive intuitive messages/revelations.

We do not know what intuition is. When we search dictionaries for the definition, they will tell us what it does, but not what it is. We all know, however, we have intuition, we know it works, and it often works miracles by providing us with important information at just the right time. It can be said Intuition is the mind's unique ability to access vital information directly from the source and make it available to us at the time when we need it most.

Ideas and opportunities could be suggested by logic and common sense but that information may or may not be right due to the mistakes the mind is known to make. Intuition you can trust and it is "heard" best when ETP (Emotional Thinking Process) is quieted down; better still – when it stops running. This happens naturally at the time of falling asleep and immediately upon waking when our thoughts are not yet running. This was how my intuition urged me to leave Navy school when I was awakened for duty shortly before 4 am.

How did my intuition know that upon graduation all the engineer-lieutenants of my class would end up at the nuclear installations in the Russian far north? Certainly, some Navy Department had already made this decision. Thus, it could have been found in the collective subconscious field for anyone's intuition to access.

How intuition finds and connects to the most essential, even critical piece of information whether in the subconscious field or any other source is a puzzle as it was in my Navy case. Intuition must be able to instantly scan the source, do it consistently and just as consistently provide us with information vital to our development and success.

This is happening at any moment in our lives when vital intuitive information is continuously sent to us. Every one of my classmates must have received the same piece of information, but they either did not hear or disregarded the message.

It happened in the past that I disregarded some intuitive messages. Without exception, each time it was a mistake.

Drawing by Anna and Nadia Balzhak in
The Incredible Adventures of Kitto

Spontaneous Irrevocable Decision

When children are brought up with Love, they are guided by Love having no knowledge of that. In an early age, nobody thinks about the great power of Love and Love's incomparable benefits. I was not an exception. Only later,

I realized how fortunate I was to have a loving Mother and Emma, our neighbor. Looking back, I saw it was not a luck but the silent Love's guidance that made my early years fly smoothly from one success to another. It was intuition given to me by my mother – the voice of Love that warned me of the pitfalls or simply moved me away from danger. At the time, I was not aware of it. When Love is realized in any age, we begin consciously steer our life in the desired direction.

There seem to be too many obstacles to surmount to accomplish the goal. However, many of these "obstacles" are inner. Nothing in the outside world can stop us from having a life of Happiness and Success. Whatever impediments and excuses we may have, most of them are of the limited mind that knows no Love. Yet, even when raised in unfortunate circumstances, each of us has the ability to make a decision and transform this misfortunate past into Love.

Decisions are present in everything we do. Usually, people do not pay much attention to their decisions and they pay even less attention to what is behind their decisions. Typically, it looks like something needs to be done and almost unaware, you decide to do it or not. You may not pay much attention to the role of decisions but decision plays a major role in your life. How to make the right decision?

Your decisions can be right but only when you are free from limitations, otherwise they are guesses. Even concepts of Love, Peace, and Freedom may become limitations, for until we realize Love we are using a "concept" of Love, which is an intellectual knowledge of Love barren of Love's power.

There is a decision and there is an irrevocable decision. There is something that is almost beyond decision and is called Spontaneous Irrevocable Decision. As you will see it further, Spontaneous Irrevocable Decision can be instantly made based on important intuitive information that suddenly enters mind as a premonition or revelation. Let us call it Revelation/Spontaneous Irrevocable Decision. It can also be made based upon the deliberate creative process: Creative/Spontaneous Irrevocable Decision. The line between Revelation/Spontaneous Irrevocable Decision and Creative/Spontaneous Irrevocable Decision is blurred. Still, the difference between these two kinds of decisions can be discerned. What is rather inexplicable is that Spontaneous Irrevocable Decision is made almost involuntarily, which is most likely – intuitively, and is a confirmation of the success at hand.

The Revelation/Spontaneous Irrevocable Decision will not be made if you disregard an intuitive information (revelation or hunch) or missed it. However, the Revelation/Spontaneous Irrevocable Decision will be made instantly if you are ready to act on information you have received. If in the past you have spent time thinking on the subject of the revelation (even indirectly and, having no prior knowledge of any revelation to come) then you may be ready to make a Revelation/Spontaneous Irrevocable Decision. With a calm mind, you will not miss a moment when a Revelation/Spontaneous Irrevocable Decision has to be made.

The cleaner is our subconscious, the more loving is our mind the easier it is for us to deal with a particular circumstance. This general rule applies to everything we do. It also can be formulated thus: the less our individuality is covered with complexities forming our personality the easier for us to receive intuitive "tipping" or "queuing", to sense a right moment and a direction. Love makes all the difference here because Love will guarantee the only beneficial results.

At 43, the doctor told Lester Levenson that he might drop dead at any time. He was about to say goodbye to life but, suddenly, he made an opposite decision – to find answers to the most puzzling questions *What is life? What is it all about?* Because these questions were in the back of Lester's mind for many years, Lester's sudden decision made in a most critical moment of his life happened to be Creative Spontaneous Irrevocable Decision that unfailingly predicts an upcoming success. Lester didn't know that but amazingly, after he nearly walked in the valley of the shadow of death, and suddenly made Spontaneous Irrevocable Decision, in 90 days he came out of it into the sunshine – into a new life of Love and Freedom.

Once, I had to see a dentist to prepare four of my teeth for crowns. As I walked in a cozy office of Dr. Bob McCracken, in Lake Isabella, I have spontaneously made an Irrevocable Decision to have no pain and use no anesthesia. When several moments later I listened to Doctor Bob explaining to me what is involved, I have found myself in a state similar to reverie. "If that's what you wish," said the Doctor, "then I will do my best to accommodate you. Are you sure you don't want Novocain?" I was okay without it.

Dr. Bob started to file my teeth – I felt no pain. When three teeth were done, Dr. Bob called in his staff to watch how the fourth tooth was prepared. He said that in more than 40 years of his practice, this is the first time when the patient wanted no anesthetic. He explained that 'shaving' a tooth under the gum is a painful procedure and added that he is amazed to watch me showing no sign of pain.

To me, there was nothing amazing about it. It felt natural, without tension and with no effort. There really was no pain, as we know it. However, when I felt some of it about to surface, I reminded pain: "Who is the boss here!" Then lovingly invited it to come up even more, and leave, disappear, evaporate. There was no effort because the effort is needed to overcome resistance and fear. Spontaneous Irrevocable Decision instantly banishes all negativity together with resistance and fear.

I heard in the past about people having root canals done without anesthetic and was convinced that I too can do it. When this conviction became unshakable, I was "made" to make a Spontaneous Irrevocable Decision, which always leads to success. In this case, the opportunity was presented immediately after a Spontaneous Irrevocable Decision was made and it was materialized in a dental chair.

Everyone occasionally has these kinds of revelations. Per his writings, Andrew Carnegie had them also. Because of his loving and relaxed state of mind, the absence of negativity and stress, Carnegie's receptivity was high, which enabled him to hear these intuitive messages, to make Spontaneous Irrevocable Decisions and seize opportunities. When the mind is rooted in Love, it attracts only beneficial opportunities.

In the case of Revelation/Spontaneous Irrevocable Decision, which situation is beyond our control, there is no initial creative process and we have no preliminary knowledge of what is coming. However, even being unexpected, Spontaneous Irrevocable Decision necessarily brings along an idea or an opportunity and enables us to execute it. We have to recognize it and act upon it. At the Navy school example, the opportunity surfaced in about few weeks when I was hospitalized with acute appendices. After surgery, I asked my doctor to help me to get out, and she did.

There is always a danger of paying no attention to the initial message, which happens to people most of the time because of their physical and emotional stress.

This happened to all of the students of my class in the Navy school – each of them either missed the message suggested to immediately leave the school or disregarded it as unimportant. When led by Love, intuitively received information and following Spontaneous Irrevocable Decision is always beneficial. I did not know this at the time. Now, many years later I can see that because of my loving upbringing I was often led by Love.

Revelation or a hunch is an intuitive message that cannot be altered by a negative mind. Intuition is the voice of Love, which is beyond the opposites.

As I am writing, I remember a 20 page "collective" letter my classmates sent me on the eve of the diploma, where each of them wrote a loving message, many of them saying they wanted to follow in my steps and leave the service. I still have the letter. We were such a close group of boys, grown together from 17 to 23 years of age.

In the Navy school (middle, below), 1958

My father (middle, below) in the Navy School of Aviation, 1934.

At 26, my father became a Soviet Navy test pilot. At 31, he died in a crash that was blamed on sabotage. When I was about 10, my mother told me a story related by the gunner who survived the crash. The day before the crash, my father submitted a report to his superiors requesting to postpone the upcoming test for two more days in order to check the plane more thoroughly. The plane was checked overnight and he was ordered to fly it the next day. Was it a premonition/Spontaneous Irrevocable Decision that made my father write the report?

After the accident, several people were found guilty of conspiracy and shot, just as it happened after every accident during Stalin's regime. It was made common knowledge in the USSR that "In the perfect Soviet society there could be no accidents except those caused by the enemies of the people." While working on Stalin miniseries many years later I have learned that out of the 84 thousand Soviet-built planes during WWII, more than 50 thousand have crashed not in combat but because of a bad workmanship caused by forced labor.

I had no thoughts of leaving the school after six years of studying and with only several months left until I was to get a diploma in engineering with the rank of the lieutenant. When I suddenly received the intuitive message advising me to walk out, it was almost shocking. My following Spontaneous Irrevocable Decision was like being struck by lightning. It was immediate and wordless. I left the school within two months, and it happened smoothly, despite all the odds.

I must admit that many times I thought of how dissatisfying my life was in the school, but I never thought of leaving. As every Spontaneous Irrevocable Decision comes together with a great opportunity, this one not only moved me out of the school, it also provided me with the opportunity to become a filmmaker, a profession I was enjoying many years.

An opportunity may seem to be great, but when not rooted in Love, it may bring a disastrous result. In the case of Adolf Hitler and Alexander the Great an opportunity led both men to premature death.

As I was led by Love, Love provided me only with beneficial opportunities. When the Red Empire fell apart, I went to Russia and secured an agreement with the Russian Ministry of Film to represent the Russian film industry in Hollywood. Together with my partner David, we created the USSR Film Service Corporation with offices at the southeast corner of Wilshire and Westwood Boulevard, in Los Angeles. Across from our building was a high-rise of the Occidental Petroleum, topped with penthouse of Armand Hammer.

Before that happened, however, David and I have been trying to establish a new business for several months until one morning I woke up with an idea to forge a deal with the Soviet film Industry. This I did without delay and our business went sky high. It was a Revelation/Spontaneous Irrevocable Decision that did it. The USSR idea came suddenly, unexpectedly, and it was instantly executed.

There is another important point about the Spontaneous Irrevocable Decisions: after it is made, fulfillment goes smoothly, unobstructed as if we are effortlessly flying in a dream. I am sure everyone has experienced flying through the air while asleep. It is an incredibly satisfying smooth flight that we are guiding by unknown means, most likely instinctively. Whatever it is and wherever it is we are flying, over the ocean or above a city, forest, desert or a field, there are no obstacles for us. Even when some obstacle suddenly arises before us, we easily flying under, above or around it, feeling even more thrilled.

It is the same with a Spontaneous Irrevocable Decision. Once it happens, everything turns into a smooth effortless flight. For several years, David and I were flying with success. We made a number of co-productions *Cops in Russia* for Fox Television; MOW *Chernobyl, the Final Warning*, *Sharks of Steel*, an Australian co-production, to *Inside the KGB*, a 90-minute special for the NBC television network. For years, we had the great press in Variety, Hollywood Reporter and LA Times…

A Creative Spontaneous Irrevocable Decision is a confirmation that our purpose is fulfilled in a mental realm and is ready to be materialized. Creative Spontaneous Irrevocable Decision is a connection to a forthcoming opportunity that is coming either immediately or sometime soon. Creative Spontaneous Irrevocable Decision's purpose is to pull us into action on the opportunity as soon as it comes. It will happen only when our purpose is fulfilled in a mental realm and is ready to be materialized.

My purpose of leaving USSR was fulfilled in the mental realm at the time when I received enlightening information on how it can be done. Simultaneously, Creative Spontaneous Irrevocable Decision presented itself and was instantly executed. An opportunity surfaced within a few days. A dissident writer George Vladimov who happened to live in my apartment building arranged for my invitation from supposed to be relatives in Israel. I did the rest.

It often looks like we are almost forced to make Spontaneous Irrevocable Decision as if we have no other choice. This happens because often unaware, we initially may fulfill a goal in the mental realm to the point it is ready to materialize, thus laying the groundwork for the Spontaneous Irrevocable Decision to happen and be executed or rejected. Usually, we execute it.

What is inexplicable is that opportunity that follows is always perfectly exercisable – exactly what we need to complete the process and start success rolling. However, as it was said earlier, it may take as long as several years for our purpose to get fulfilled in the mental realm because we didn't do our homework right, thus being not yet ready to start success rolling. During this test by the time you may retrospect, find any weak links in the chain of our homework and reinforce them.

Spontaneous Irrevocable Decision happens only when success is at hand. The moment it happens, we are effortlessly driven to success as if by an invisible force.

"We look upon our financial position with a mix of disbelief and humility, never having dreamed that we would be in this situation. Our backgrounds are similar to that of many Americans. We each had a solid middle-class upbringing with an emphasis on values, work ethic, and social responsibility. We each attended public secondary school and worked our way through private universities. And, of course, we dreamed of one day being "rich," in the way that all young people fantasize about having everything they want.

"To our great surprise, we now fit that very elementary label."

Laura & John Arnold/*The Giving People*

"The journey which began in poverty somehow led to my name's inclusion on the Richest Americans list for several years running.

"We progressed from being leveraged to the eyeballs to realizing a degree of wealth of which we had never dared to dream, always with the understanding that it was not ours to keep. Through hard work, luck at the right times, and a determination to succeed, we built a company which filled our coffers with money intended for others."
John and Karen Huntsman/*The Giving People*

"In 2004, I had the extraordinary opportunity to help create Facebook, which has grown to connect half a billion people, dramatically increasing communication and transparency worldwide. As a result of Facebook's success, I've earned financial capital beyond my wildest expectations. Today, I view that reward not as personal wealth, but as a tool with which I hope to bring even more benefit to the world."
Dustin Moskovitz and Cari Tuna/*The Giving People*

It is entirely different from the haphazard thinking process that has many directions and no purpose. Still, Spontaneous Irrevocable Decision is a decision, which may be likened to a situation as when we have an empty tank and make the decision to stop at the gas station. Do we have a choice? We can choose not to stop, but how far can we get?

Even when our past is not yet transformed into Love, Spontaneous Irrevocable Decisions will happen, bypassing both, the conscious and the subconscious mind. This happens because our mind's unknown 95% is infinitely more powerful and capable compared to the known 5%, thus making the Spontaneous Irrevocable Decision the thing to bypass our entire subconscious archive with all its negative influence. However, it can only happen when there is no negativity regarding the project/goal in question. This is why some outwardly negative people still become successful: they harbor no fears or doubts, no negativity about their goals.

Everyone who has risen from rags to riches has experienced Spontaneous Irrevocable Decision despite their subconscious containing negativity. Talent, powerful imagination, as well as the absence of negativity regarding the goal, did the job.

When there is no Love, ignorance takes over, expressing itself in greed, anger, envy… and becomes some one's guiding force. The result is 994 mass shooting in 1004 days as of October 2015. This is not an American "gun crisis", for the guns have little to do with it. It is an American social crisis. Police brutality and racism; illegal wars and bombing hospitals in Iraq, Afghanistan, and Libya; the murder of innocent people cynically called "collateral damage"; hypocritical presidents, fraudulent administration, inept lawmakers, and judges… all this is caused by the absence of Love, by the none loving upbringing.

In our busy lives, we do not pay much attention to it, but whatever success we have, big or small, it is always preceded by the Spontaneous Irrevocable Decision. It moves us to the realm of accomplishment and will always have our purpose accomplished whether it is for good or wrong ends. The "wrong ends success" is inevitably devoid of Love.

Spontaneous Irrevocable Decision is a state of absolute knowing that eliminates or moves us beyond even traces of the negativity in relation to the goal. In relation to our fundamental purpose of Happiness and Success, when Creative Spontaneous Irrevocable Decision happens we are instantly embedded into an inexplicable state of knowing beyond any doubt, beyond all evidence to the contrary, that we have made it, we are already in our world of Happiness and Success.

I call it Spontaneous Irrevocable Decision, but it also may be called an affirmation of the completion of inner work that starts our flight to Success.

As in the case of Andrew Carnegie, whose initial life's purpose was $300 for his family, there is no limit to growth. After his initial success when Carnegie presented his mother with the horse-driven carriage, which was a great accomplishment at the time, he began his rapid ascension to unparalleled success.

When Spontaneous Irrevocable Decision is rooted in our essence – Love – it assures nature's positive intention. However, more often than not Creative Spontaneous Irrevocable Decision is squandered by a selfish mind that knows no Love. When Love is obscured, we may be driven by wrong intentions fueled by greed, anger, vengeance, etc. Nonetheless, Spontaneous Irrevocable Decision will still guarantee results but these results may be disastrous. When Love is our guide, the Creative Spontaneous Irrevocable Decision will guarantee only beneficial results.

Jim Uny was brought up with Love. At seventeen he said to his parents that high school is enough of an education, that he is determined to be a millionaire. This Spontaneous

Irrevocable Decision has propelled Jim fast to Success. At eighteen, he was driving a school bus, then – the truck. Soon, he owned a truck, and a little later he was in a trucking business. He was 35 years old, when he made his first million, hauling rocks.

Soon he had several businesses running, and a park full of heavy machinery: trucks, cranes, bulldozers, trailers... On his own, he learned how to operate and fix every piece of equipment. Later, this equipment came in handy in the Sequoia Wilderness, 40 miles away from the nearest town of Kernville.

When Jim was a small boy, his father was often taking him to the Sequoia National Forest. He fell in love with the beauty of Sierra Nevada Mountains and decided that this is where he would live.

I met Jim when he was living in a large beautiful house that he built with logs of Canadian yellow pine, and only one other person's help – his wife Gloria. It stood in a valley overgrown with whispering pines. There are a waterfall and a brook running gaily nearby: a 320-acre estate of nature's paradise in the heart of the Sequoias.

Jim always wanted to fly a helicopter. Now was his time. He was in his late forties, when half a mile away from his house, single-handedly he blasted, crushed and moved tons of rock, and built a professional helipad (also used by firefighters, police, and emergency) then, together with his wife, he built a hangar and a large machine shop. This was at the same time when I moved to the Sequoias; I saw it all and even wielded a pick hammer, it was very hard to handle.

Whatever Jim does, must be perfect. He has built my house and solar system, and today, seventeen years later it is all in perfect shape. If someone does work for him, it must be as perfect as if he did it himself; it is not easy for some people to handle.

What is significant about this man is his unwavering determination to accomplish his dream and to do it entirely on his own. The strength of the confidence is the key. Jim has an unshakable confidence in himself that has aided him to literally move mountains, and do it all with his own two hands.

At the end of a 25-mile dead-end road, there is a summer camp in the Sequoias for underprivileged children from Los Angeles and Bakersfield. The camp is completely off the grid. Jim created and installed a telephone system there. He is taking care of all the camp's needs: their electric system, water pump and three tanks he had installed, clearing property, logging, repairs, and construction. When a winter-storm damaged the road, Jim repaired the road on his own initiative and with no charge to the camp.

Jim's is a big loving heart that enabled him to build his own beautiful world and he is enjoying living and working in it. He is a rare example of success at building his life's dream entirely on his own. It was a rooted in Love Creative Spontaneous Irrevocable Decision, made by Jim when he was just 17 years old, that did it. However, before it was made, Jim often thought about his future life being independent and rich. Many people dream of an independent and rich life, but only a few are able to create it. Only those who are led by Love enjoy Happiness. When I asked Jim what would happen to his properties, machinery, and so on, when he is gone..., he smiled: "I took care of it so that people will enjoy it for many years to come."

Creative Spontaneous Irrevocable Decision on any subject can be made when we are thoroughly released, especially on the subject in question. For obvious reasons, we can plan neither Revelation/Spontaneous Irrevocable Decision nor Creative Spontaneous Irrevocable Decision. It arrives suddenly. It comes on its own because of growth; it comes almost as a surprise. However, this thought of surprise is only a vague interpretation of something that comes swiftly and wordlessly.

Spontaneous Irrevocable Decisions happens just like a flash of lightning. Like Freedom, it happens spontaneously. The subject of the Spontaneous Irrevocable Decision may be elaborated upon for quite some time, and a conscious decision could be made on this subject but it will not be a Spontaneous Irrevocable Decision. It will be just another decision that may be right or wrong.

A Spontaneous Irrevocable Decision will always be right in the sense that it will start a process of fulfillment of your purpose. It will always be greatly beneficial to others and yourself when your past is transformed into Love and you are led by Love.

My friend Yakov told me about the opportunity of leaving the USSR for Israel then the only country where immigration was permitted but was extremely difficult to achieve. When Yakov explained some details, my decision to leave the USSR was immediate. First, I was excited, and then at some point in the conversation, I suddenly felt very peaceful. At that moment, I knew, without a word, that I have already left Russia. I collected the necessary papers, and after submitting them, I received an exit visa in two months, which was unheard of.

Today, I know it was a Spontaneous Irrevocable Decision that did it. I must say I was fascinated with American and British producers and enjoyed working with them. They were like people from another planet to me. America was an enigma; without having any knowledge of the country I had a strong feeling it is great. However, I never seriously thought of leaving the USSR.

In each case, Spontaneous Irrevocable Decision has completely changed my life for the better. In each case, there was no thinking, analyzing or figuring it out. Also, there was no desire. Spontaneous Irrevocable Decision is made somewhere in another dimension, in the realm of certainty, beyond desire. There was always a calm conviction present: "It is done." That conviction was present despite a total lack of knowledge of what would happen and how it would happen. There were no worries, no concerns. I knew nothing then about the all-conquering power of Love. Yet, because my mother brought up my sister and me with Love, we were loving people. Spontaneous Irrevocable Decision will always be beneficial when our purpose is rooted in Love when we are led by Love.

When the subconscious is not yet cleansed, it is impossible to find the key to making the right decision. By the right decision, I mean a decision that will directly or indirectly contribute to inner growth and Success. People often make "right" decisions that benefit themselves but may cause damage to others. Many "right" decisions, harmonious with selfish purpose of the decision-makers resulted in disastrous wars. This is an example of "right" decisions having been made for the wrong purpose that caused harm to other people, and contributed to a deeper ignorance of the decision makers.

To increase the probability of Spontaneous Irrevocable Decision you need to "open a window" into the present moment and keep it open. To open this window, you will need to do the same steps: to learn to watch your mind and to clean your past of negativity. To keep the "window" open, it is necessary to watch the mind, to keep letting go/transforming to Love any ripple of negativity that is encountered. To keep the "window" open means to live in the present.,

You will be tempted to look for opportunities and may decide to pursue some, but you will be searching in the dark. Whatever you will do prior to the Spontaneous Irrevocable Decision may work or it may not work in the long run, even if it looks like a "good" opportunity. It may even work, and you may become successful. However, there is a much bigger chance, however, for a true Success not to happen. Only Spontaneous Irrevocable Decision rooted in Love confirms (true) Success.

The above reminded me of the *Bardo Thodol, the Tibetan Book of the Dead* where *Bardo Thodol* means hearing with one's heart. It says that at the time of death every human being must pass through the realm called Bardo. It makes no difference whether this book is true or fantasy because it makes a powerful example of negativity affecting our daily life, for Bardo Thodol is also a book of life.

Whatever fears and horrors the Bardo traveler imagined and/or experienced during his/her life, it is vividly reproduced and greatly exaggerated in the Bardo realm. This stunning illusion of reality deceives one into believing it is real, tempting him or her to act accordingly, consequently making one mistake after another, thus getting completely mesmerized.

The Tibetans say that only the wise know those negative images are not real and will not succumb to the illusion.

You know the truth. Do not be deceived by the misleading "reality" of the human world. Play the game of life by the rules of the wise. When you do, Spontaneous Irrevocable Decision – your confirmation of the smooth ride to Success – will happen.

From the age of six to about ten, when classes at school were over, our neighbor Emma was looking daily after my younger sister and me as our mother was working late. Very unusual for those Soviet times, Emma, a daughter of the Tsar's deputy minister of education, was left alive and in possession of a large library. Communists killed Emma's parents and all her relatives shortly after the revolution. Emma's only son died in WWII. Her husband, an engineer, was exiled for 25 years to the Bering Strait separating Alaska from Siberia. Emma lived alone.

Gentle and kind, Emma became a second mother to my sister and me. It was 1945. A devastating WWII has just ended and there was a shortage of everything even in Moscow. Yet, my sister and I felt nothing of it as our mother and Emma created for us a very happy environment.

When at school, I could not wait to get to Emma's, and to those beautiful volumes bound in dark brown leather. I am truly indebted to the loving, caring woman who introduced me to *Robinson Crusoe*, *Treasure Island*, *The World Travels* series, and other books that awakened in me a burning desire to see the world.

Like most Russian people, we were poorer than a church mouse and no one in Stalin's Russia would ever dream of traveling abroad. In 1945, it was as impossible as to travel to the moon. However, thanks to Emma and my imagination, I was traveling! At school, I was drawing tall ships under my command, at Emma's I was dying to get to another chapter of *Robinson Crusoe,* at night in my dreams I was fighting pirates or fighting together with them against British navy.

It took 15 years for my 'travel' desire to start materializing. My travels began in Russia when I made my first documentary in Siberia. Then I volunteered to make films for Sakhalin Television channel, at the far Russian East, north of Japan. Afterward, for several years I was enjoying traveling while making documentaries all over Russia. Now, over 50 years later I am still traveling thanks to that Spontaneous Irrevocable Decision I made at an early age.

You have no idea how frustrating it was to want a car in the Soviet Russia and had no hope, no chance of getting one. I was 23. As I was crossing Gorky Street in Moscow, I saw a Moskvich car parked on the other side of the street. As a huge magnet, it seemed to be pulling at me. I remember the scene as if it happened yesterday: brightly lit by a huge street light, it was a beautiful station wagon car: dark blue with red leather seats: everything one would want to have at 23.

I saw similar cars before, but this time it was different. As I stood there drunk with its beauty, not able to move, seemingly for no reason I felt very happy, like a child with a new toy. I had even imagined driving this car. An incredibly convincing thought crossed my mind "It's yours", and as instantly, it was gone. "Stupid!" I remember saying to myself, "it's not yours." But that initial feeling "It's yours", remained. As I was walking away, I remember saying "Not a chance!" And the whole thing was forgotten.

Today I know it was a Spontaneous Irrevocable Decision made at the time of the encounter that assured my possession of the exact same car. It was that "not a chance!" doubt that had delayed my ownership of the car for seven years. Here is the story. Three years later, I was offered a lucrative job at the newly opened film department at the Novosti Press Agency. It was an exciting job as I was filming documentaries for British and American producers. I completely forgot about my dream car, partly because the agency's car was always at my disposal.

Time flew. One day, while filming for Encyclopedia Britannica in St. Peterburg I saw a group of clergy in a lobby of my hotel Astoria. Without giving it any thought, I approached one of the priests and out of blue asked him if he would be interested in making a film for his church. Ivan was his name, wrote his telephone number on a piece of newspaper and gave it to me. He happened to be father superior of one of only four active monasteries in the Soviet Union, intended to prove to foreign tourists that Soviet people are enjoying religious freedom.

Like in some great adventure story, my friend Evgeni and I were secretly contracted to produce a color 35 mm underground documentary film about the monks' life and their struggles during the Soviet regime. It was over 15 years before the Red Empire went down, and Ivan felt its end was near. Sadly, he did not live to enjoy that day.

The film was completed in about 12 months and received a great amount of money we never expected to get. If caught making an unauthorized film for the church, we would end up with 25 years of hard labor in Siberia or a far Russian North. However, for some reason, I felt no fear, despite Ivan's warning that the KGB operatives in civilian clothing were always present in the monastery. The reason I learned much later about. It was my loving attitude towards people and life that warded off danger.

Ivan ordered to put our creation in airtight metal containers and to hide in the monastery's catacombs, where the saints were buried for over six hundred years. To my knowledge, it is still there.

As I stood, waiting for my car at the delivery station, suddenly, a dark blue Moskvich car rolled in a station wagon with the red leather seats. A driver came out and gave me keys. At that moment, I remembered my encounter on Gorky Street, seven years past.

Did you notice how unexpectedly a great opportunity presented itself? Though I completely forgot my encounter with the Moskvich car, the subconscious remembered it. A great shock of that loving encounter had made a deep groove in the subconscious with Spontaneous Irrevocable Decision, yet I knew nothing of it until many years later.

Do you still not believe in the creative power of the mind, as well as the treacheries role that doubt and fear play in delaying or destroying your goals! I knew nothing about the process of creation, but as you could see, the law of creation works regardless of our knowledge of it. Yet, having the treasure of *the right knowledge*, we put ourselves in the driver's seat of our Destiny car.

The following story took place during the filming of my first documentary film. I was traveling three months in Eastern Siberia together with a group of 11 young men along the majestic Sayan Mountains, crossing Siberia from North to the southern border with China.

It was the end of August; the winds had ceased in the high mountain country of Siberia; Indian summer set in. Each day, the sun rose later and set a little earlier, with twilight lingering into the night. The whole day was ablaze with the sunshine.

Autumn came unexpectedly. Its first chilly night colored the high grass of the riverbanks in yellow. That day, we moored the rafts by a gently sloping shore of the peaceful river and indulged in berries. It was a great season for all sorts of sweet and sour berries.

An old man appeared nearby. He wore a gray mustache, a shock of gray hair, and a long gray beard, covering his chest and shoulders. He carried a large old-fashioned berry-basket in his hand. The Monk, as we called him, invited us to rest for the night in his house, about a mile away.

Made of huge logs, the house stood peacefully beneath old firs, overgrown with a red berry bush, undisturbed by the passage of time. With its narrow windows, the house looked out on a serene lake called Silver. With a blackened roof set almost on the ground, the nearby bathhouse was hardly visible, hidden in tall grass and bushes. We enjoyed that place immensely. The night was spent in conversation.

The son of Siberian Governor, Gregory was born in 1887. He was raised by his grandmother the Duchess Galanskaya and educated in London. However, Gregory's heart was not with the world. With his father's permission and grandmother's blessing, Gregory left the world in search of God.

The 1917 Communist revolution found him in the Orthodox Christian Monastery of Solovki. The seven hundred years old monastery stood at an inhospitable island in the cold White Sea of the Russian far north.

"It is a wondrous place," Gregory said. "Eternity dwells there within magnificent cathedrals and tall churches."

The communists converted Solovki into a concentration camp. Two years later, Gregory escaped from the island and wandered to the Siberian Taiga. When he first happened upon the house, it could hardly be seen, overgrown with vegetation. Inside, the house was immaculate, as if the owner had stepped out but a moment ago.

No one ever came to Gregory's strange place – only wolves, bears, and foxes. Several times a Siberian tiger passed by. Gregory believed it was still around since he saw neither bears nor wolves nearby. I was amazed by the man and envious of his tranquil way of life. He made such a grand impression on me. At that moment, I was convinced beyond the shadow of the doubt this is how I should live. At the time, I did not know I was led by Love. I did not think about Love until I came to America. Only then, many years later, I realized that the happy upbringing by the loving parents is the most precious gift one could ever receive.

That longing to live in seclusion did not disappear. For many years, I forgot about it but it was engraved deeply in my subconscious, and almost 40 years later I found myself living in the heart of Sequoia National Forest, in the mountains, over 40 miles away from the nearest town of Kernville, with my surroundings incredibly resembling Eastern Siberia.

Though I am long time used to the mind's creative "miracles", this one was quite shocking when I suddenly realized a forty-year span between the time when my subconscious was impregnated with a great loving desire, and its materialization.

There are many inexplicable things in life. The mechanism of *The Spontaneous Irrevocable Decision* is still inexplicable. Love's amazing power and ability to do only good, to create only beneficial circumstances are also inexplicable. Would it make any difference if we know the cause of this benevolence? Because Love is an extension of Infinite Intelligence in the human world, the cause of the Love's power lies with Infinite Intelligence that created the Universes. Does it sound anti-intellectual? Then, listen to Einstein:

The scientist's religious feeling takes the form of rapturous amazement at the harmony of natural law that reveals an intelligence of such superiority that, in comparison with it, all the systematic thinking of human beings is an utterly insignificant reflection. This feeling is a guiding principle of his life and work.

Our Solar system is such a precise and beautiful arrangement that can only be designed intelligently with Love. Yet, Infinite Intelligence does not interfere in a life of the Universe and humanity. Though it is beyond understanding, Infinite Intelligence is present everywhere, its hints can be comprehended in deep meditation. It can also be "sensed" intuitively. Our universe is born and is nourished with Love, but it is not controlled or possessed by its creator. We are free to imagine and create a life of our choosing. The universe and humanity are free to evolve, to take the best possible course because it is designed to evolve to perfection.

What can be more joyous than the realization of being an integral part of the Creator, which means – being the Creator?

Skepticism blocks the creative process. People are used to believing only in what they see. *Imagination* is nothing but fantasy to those who shuffle through life unwilling to use their great resource of the mind's creativity.

Happiness is Love that knows no skepticism. Love and Happiness should be taught in schools. It could be done when teachers were to learn the path of Love, even if they do not walk the path.

Hurghada, Egypt

Selection

-Habit is a substitute for Happiness.

-We choose a habit because we do not know how to find Happiness.

-Love knows no mental effort. Because Love is beyond effort, one who realized Love knows no stress.

-Love and hate do not coexist.

-When hating, we are punishing ourselves.

-Love is not justifying, judging or criticizing; it is witnessing and seeing the truth.

-From the time when Lester understood he could transform his negative past into Love, it took him only 30 days to realize Love.

-True Success is beneficial to its creator as well as to others. The greater is Success, the more people it will benefit.

-A success, created without Love is a handicapped success, regardless of its size.

-When Love is not yet realized we believe that our judgments are right. It is an erroneous belief because judgment is of the limited mind and is itself an error.

-The one who is influenced by the negative past cannot see the truth because hidden in the subconscious negativity distorts vision. Unaware, this person would keep missing truth and... make mistakes

-Those who were brought up with Love and those who discovered Love have every opportunity at finding Happiness and (true) Success.

-There can be no Happiness without Love.

-The less our unique individuality is covered with acquired personality the easier it is for us to receive an intuitive advice on how to act in each circumstance.

-Not having preconceived knowledge of Love is *the right knowledge* and a good start. Having preconceived ideas about Love may be likened to a disease. First, realized that you are sick. Then, move towards *the right knowledge* of Love and a good health.

-Entertainment attracts people; they enjoy it. However, *the right knowledge* that points to Love seems monotonous. When you look for Love, there is nothing to see. When you realize it, it is boundless.

-In a business world, when there is no Love, competition and connections rule a success. A true Success knows no competition.

-It is common for a business person to neglect family. When Love is the leader, both business and family benefit.

-A media pays much attention to anything but Love because the ignorant mind fears Love.

-Choosing Love means choosing Happiness and (true) Success. The moment one chooses Love is the moment when one's life and business begin to thrive.

-When children are raised with Love, they would have a greater chance at finding Happiness and Success. It is the same with business: conducted with Love, it will thrive in (true) Success.

-When a relationship does not grow into Love, it becomes a burden. It is the same with business. When business is conducted in the absence of Love, it soon becomes a burden. The bigger is a business the bigger the burden.

-A success without Love will bring only a temporary satisfaction and... misery.

-An indifference is a cover for a hidden negativity (greed, animosity, envy, anger, etc.). When Love is realized, indifference is gone. What left, is a loving mind.

-Witnessing is impartial. There is a difference between being indifferent and impartial. An impartial witnessing is compassionate and understanding.

-Being an impartial witness, one can see through people and events.

-There is no selfishness in the desire to succeed. Every child is born to succeed. Selfishness is a refusal to share success.

-With Love, there is always a rewarding way.

-When Love enters our heart, the mind is no longer in charge; it becomes a tool. When the mind is no longer in charge, we make fewer or no mistakes because Love knows no mistakes. A mistake may happen only when we sidetrack, slip off the Love's point of view and choose the mind's suggestion instead.

-"How can I do what I love and be paid to support my family that requires about $100,000/year?" It can be done either with pushing or it can be achieved with Love that will also bestow Happiness upon you.

-Love is neither negative nor positive… it is compassionate, kind, accepting and understanding.

-Under average circumstances, a mind control is an impossible task because the mind is silently influenced by the subconscious. To achieve control of the mind, the subconscious must be purified.

-Uncontrolled mind creates chaos. When the mind is led by Love, it creates a life of Happiness and Success.

-When led by Love, the mind does not need to be controlled because Love is in control.

-Many problems are rooted in not loving the self. We must eliminate every negativity we feel about our body and mind. Our Love of self must be total and unconditional. Look directly into your eyes in the mirror, tell yourself "I love you (your name) unconditionally and this body as it is." Transform into Love to yourself every negative thought and feeling as they surface.

-Affirmations are a good help in the beginning of transformation process:

"I trust the power and intelligence of Love."
"In the universe of Love, all is whole and perfect."
"My Life is a great adventure; I love and enjoy its every instant."
"I am born to succeed."
"Love guides me to the right place at the right time…"

-When there is no Love, the subconscious is in charge and, regardless of the size of success, it will create problems by causing the mind to make mistakes. The mind can be effortlessly "controlled" only by Love.

-You are successful in business, entertainment, as a student or a teacher… Yet, your success did not bring you Happiness. You experience only glimpses of Happiness, which is not Happiness but a temporary satisfaction. In between these glimpses is irritation, misery, frustration, fear – a rainbow of negative emotions that Lester calls the AGFLAP (apathy, greed, fear, lust, anger, and (false) pride).

-When you make love you are satisfied, when your partner is not responsive you are miserable; when your children obedient you are satisfied, when they do not behave you are irritated; it is the same with your employees, associates, business partners, and friends: when you are in agreement you are satisfied, when agreement is violated you are angry. Unaware, you created causes of this rollercoaster in the past, often in childhood. Now they are hiding deep in the subconscious. You cannot see these causes.

-"I loved President Kennedy," says Val, a woman in her seventies. "When I found out what he really was I lost all respect for the man; I hate this man!" Like many others, I used to believe people get wiser when they get older. Unfortunately, this was an erroneous belief. There are many seniors in the US government but most of them grew clever and cunning, not wiser. Whether rich or poor, famous or unknown, most people do not have enough wisdom to realize the danger of negativity. Some people even call it "human" to experience negative emotions and thoughts because they cannot imagine how to live without it.

John Kennedy was not a wise man either. Wisdom will never start a war. It will never authorize the use of Agent Orange, the deadliest chemical, in the war. Neither would it approve a free administering of the opium to the US soldiers in Vietnam… Yet, hate could take place only in the absence of Love.

-When Love purifies our inner vision, we begin to enjoy every instant.

-For one who realized Love there is no difference between "small" or "big" Success, it is a shared Success.

-With Love, we let events take their course.

-Love is synonymous with Happiness.

-The mind can be either led by the subconscious to mistakes and frustration or it can be led by Love to Happiness and Success.

-With Love, we are the world.

-We did such a good job at adapting and hiding negativity, it would require an irrevocable decision and determination to "bring us back" to the reality of Love.

-Love is wisdom.

-Positive thinking, when it is "inborn", is a wonderful way to live. Yet, when we try to be positive, it becomes a torment.

-With Love, we do not seek and hope… we allow things happen.

-*Transformation* of the negative past into Love is a skill. Like any other skill, it must be learned. It is learned with practice.

-When Love leads, people follow.

-Every success is created with confidence and self-esteem. Yet, if not rooted in Love, a success eventually will begin to work against us with stress and anxiety.

-Love knows no holiness, morality or justice; it knows Happiness.

-Guilt has no real purpose yet, people are holding on to the guilt throughout their lives... A man was captured during the war by the enemy and tortured to cooperation. After the war, he became a politician. Yet, that guilt created by his capture did not dissolve by itself; it made the man a saber-rattler. His position gives him a momentary satisfaction in destroying others yet, hate has turned his life into an utter misery.

- When she was young, a woman lost her child through a negligence. 40 years later, she still cannot forgive herself. Her deep feeling of guilt made her irritable and angry, causing her to ruin relationships and lose jobs. She believes her guilt is a deserved punishment, that she has no right to be happy. Love knows no punishment.

- With Love, Success is always true.

-Our future is shaped by the three elements: thinking/imagination, emotions, and subconscious influence. The subconscious influence is hidden from view.

-With Love, we experience the mystery of life. Without Love, we are surviving in a dreamland.

-If you were repeatedly told by your parents, "you are no good" it could have resulted in criticizing and blaming yourself, in procrastination and laziness, and in an inferiority complex. Love will cure you.

- You may repeat it an infinite number of times: "The past has no power over me" yet, it will keep exerting great influence over you because just by repeating the words it is impossible to eradicate hidden causes. Affirmation can be a helpful aid to *transformation,* no more than that.

-If releasing technique can be compared to remodeling an apartment, *transformation* can be likened to moving from the apartment to the beautiful house.

-Love gets her way without pushing and striving.

-Love does not take sides.

-With Love, we are content to be ourselves.

-The best diet is a mental diet.

-The big problem is the same for all people: the absence of Love.

-Love is like a well; it is inexhaustible.

-With Love, we do not crave money and security; we have what we need.

-An incredible intelligence within us can be expressed in full only with the power of Love.

-The way of Love is the only way to (true) Happiness and Success.

-Love is effortlessly nourishing all things.

-Love has all the answers.

-Love is the answer.

-There are no impediments to the realization of Love except conditioning and resistance created by the negative past. We need to accept it and transform into loving ourselves.

-To love yourself means <u>always</u> to be lovingly supportive of yourself.

-Once you come to love yourself, you will forever enjoy this affair.

-It is hard to correct problems while having the biggest problem of all: the absence of Love.

-Always, begin your day with gratitude for everything you have.

-The absence of Love is the only cause of inequality.

-When negativity is gone, mind falls quiet. When the mind is naturally at ease, the body easily takes care of itself.

-When Love is realized we are in the flow, enjoying each present moment, and letting the future to take care of itself.

-Craving Love realization is an obstacle as it emphasizes the lack of realization. Instead, there should be a conviction that realization is at hand.

-If you still doubt Love's supreme power that brings Happiness and Success, make your own simple research. You will learn that every human problem is rooted in the absence of Love. What does the following tell you: Seventy-five percent of all American children knew no Love in their childhood…? How many politicians are honest and sincere? Only a few. The underlying reason is an unhappy upbringing, the absence of Love. As a rule, the wrongdoers had no love in their childhood and there is no Love present in their adult life. Examine your own life to learn that mistakes you made were made because you were guided by the mind, not Love.

-Happiness and Success are everyone's birthright.

-Those who are not kind, honest and sincere have been "conditioned" this way in the absence of Love.

-With Love, you are *the lion that moves alone:* you are independent of the others' opinions and judgments. You have everything you need when you need it. You know what is necessary for you to know to create a life of Happiness and Success.

-When you are open to Love you are one with Love.

-Talent is not the true heart of Success, Love is.

-Success without Love is like a red color for a bull: it keeps aggravating the successful by reminding of the absence of Happiness.

-The life's moment not enjoyed is the moment lost. Fully enjoy the wonder and beauty of each instant.

-Love has no attachments.

-With Love, we see with inner vision.

-When Love is realized, we stop following… anybody.

-Love rejects no one.

-When we unconditionally accept the world, we are in Love.

-Do you still want to improve the world?

-This world is designed to evolve to perfection.

-Weapons are the tools of fools.

-Love knows no enemy.

-An inner peace is the Love's chief value.

-Infinite Intelligence is there for everyone to use. Begin with the Love-realization and you will be shown the next step.

-When there is no Love, we create deities.

You are welcome to continue this list:

Bibliography

Andrew Carnegie *Autobiography*
Andrew Carnegie *The Gospel of Wealth*
Dr. Jack Lee Rosenberg *Body, Self, Soul and Sustaining Integration*
Lao Tsu, *Tao Te Ching*, Vintage Books, 1972
Levenson, Lester, *The Final Step to Freedom*
Lloyd, Virginia, *Choose Freedom,* Freedom Publications, Phoenix, Arizona, 1983
Napoleon Hill, *The Law of Success*
Price, A. & Wong Mou-Lam, *The Sutra of Hui Neng*, Hyperion Press, Inc., Westport, Connecticut, 1973
Red Pine, translator, *Zen Teaching of Bodhidharma,* North Point Press, San Francisco, 1989
Vivekananda, Swami, *The Yoga and Other Works,* Ramakrishna-Vivekananda Center, New York, 1996
Wood, Ernest, *Zen Dictionary*, Charles E Tuttle Company, Tokyo, Japan, 1988

About the Author

Yuri Spilny was born in Vladivostok, Russia. His life has been varied and unusual. After six years in Navy School, he decided it was not for him. "When awakening for a duty, I was hit with this," he says, "Now walk out of here!" And I left the School just three months before graduation." He went to Moscow Film School and began a successful career of a documentary filmmaker. Traveling the world, he produced over 70 documentary films on a wide variety of subjects. He lectured at the University of Economics and Moscow State University on *Awareness, Responsibility,* and *Freedom*. In North America, he studied comparative religious philosophies, practiced meditation. "I always knew," he says, "that my destiny was to write," and he wrote *The Incredible Adventures of Kitto*, beautifully illustrated trilogy of fairytales emphasizing to young readers "every child is born to succeed." His most recent books are *Gates of the Dead,* a spiritual novel; *Freedom Technique: Path to Awareness and Love* and *The Lion Moves Alone* (see: Yuri Spilny at Amazon.com/books). Yuri lives in Sequoia National Forest, California.

gratitude@wildblue.net

Other books by the author

"This book is for your heart... In this book, Yuri makes you ask yourself... Can I learn to trust something more than my own mind? Like Alice in Wonderland and her steps through the mirror, am I really so close and still not seeing: 'IT' has been within me all the time? Why do I insist on hanging on to my mind's guidance when it really knows so little about Life? Can I quiet my mind long enough to give my heart the first say in the rest of my life's journey?
"I have found this to be a priceless exercise. And I am now embracing this journey that I have always been on but for the first time with an embracing of no limits to the volume of love I can contain. I've turned the mirror around and I see my inner self."

Jill Sloan, Kernville, CA

Freedom Technique: Path to Awareness and Love
Kindle: http://www.amazon.com/kindle/dp/B006XZZM0E
Paperback: https://www.createspace.com/3694994

First, comes desire, it is followed by hope, by disappointment and suffering; then comes search. Search discovers Love. With Love comes the simplicity of being in the "now" and joy that melts down desires. Your mind is educated when your entire past is transformed to Love. When it happens, Love becomes the leader and the educated, aware mind follows its intuitive lead.

Kindle: http://www.amazon.com/dp/B00GEKWLQQ
Paperback: https://www.createspace.com/4298483

You can have, be, and do whatever you will or desire. The only thing stopping you is the accumulation of negative thoughts and feelings, which you are subconsciously holding. Remove these, and you remove the blocks to your accomplishing whatever you wish in life. Remove these, and you will find love, happiness, and joy beyond your wildest dreams. Remove these, and you are Free.

Love is an absolutely necessary ingredient on the path. To get full Realization, we must increase our love until it is complete.

Lester Levenson

Lester's Wisdom in two volumes available in Kindle format and paperback.

The Incredible Adventures of Kitto
Set of three books (8.5"x 11") with over 80 original illustrations in **Full Color**

A set of three original books is available at www.bookstoenjoy.com
E-books, as well as softcover books, are available at Amazon.com

THE MIDWEST BOOK REVIEW

The Children's Bookwatch

An official Newsletter of
The Midwest Book Review
http://www.execpc.com/~mbr/bookwatch/

The Incredible Adventures of Kitto
Yuri Spilny
Bookstoenjoy.com
HC1, Box 106, Kernville, CA 93238
yuri@bookstoenjoy.com

Beautifully illustrated with more than eighty original watercolors by Anna and Nada Balzhak, "The Incredible Adventures of Kitto" is a wondrous trilogy of fairytale stories that emphasize to their young readers "every child is born to succeed".

Sorceress's Spell (1-892316-00-5) follows ten-year-old Kitto as he incurs the wrath of the wicked Milady. Escaping Milady's powers via a flying dragon and aided by the good Fairy Sambhava, Kitto creates four magical toys who become Kitto's best friends. The Toynapers (01-3) finds Kitto bringing his toys to participate in The Greatest Toy Show on Earth, where Princess Daisy falls in love with them and her father makes Kitto his royal toy master -- only to see Kitto end up falsely accused of a terrible crime, convicted and imprisoned. River of Fire (02-1) begins with a breathtaking escape for the now blind Kitto through the services of his good friend, the flying dragon. Aided by Fairy Sambhava once again, Kitto and his toys travel to the enchanted River of Fire. Together they encounter and overcome great dangers. Eventually, they reach the Pearl Palace of a terrible wizard and obtain a very special treasure.

A highly recommended fairytale trilogy.

James A. Cox, Editor-in-Chief.

"...Their love was not of this world. They knew nothing except great love for each other. It was all they had, and they didn't want anything else." The Magician fell silent, looking at distant mountains veiled in the blue mist of a dying day. From that far-away mountain country or maybe from that ancient realm where unearthly love had once bloomed, a flock of birds flew in, as if greeting the Magician...

... A timeless, enlightening adventure, a flight from grief in search of happiness.

This story is spun by a loving and creative writer, but it is the subject of the story – the meaning of love, life and death – and its treatment that set the book apart. *Gates of the Dead* has importance both timely and timeless and contains much practical wisdom that can be taken at many levels depending on the reader's receptivity. As a contribution to the subject of Love, it is unique among the books on the subject.

> Prof. Olga Volkogonova, Department of Philosophy of Science. Moscow State University

This story offers greater insight into the little voice inside all of us that speaks directly to and through our hearts. There are no accidents to love. And fleeting as it may feel at times when bound to this earth's rules, it is truly limitless on the other side.
.

> Jill Sloan, Kernville, California

Paperback: https://www.createspace.com/4416121
Also available on Kindle at Amazon.com

Printed in Dunstable, United Kingdom